PERGAMON GENERAL PSYCHOLOGY SERIES

Editors: Arnold P. Goldstein, *Syracuse University*
Leonard Krasner, *SUNY, Stony Brook*

Child Behavior Modification:
A Manual for Teachers, Nurses, and Parents

PGPS-24

Child Behavior Modification:
A Manual for Teachers, Nurses, and Parents

LUKE S. WATSON, Jr.
Columbus State Institute, Columbus, Ohio

PERGAMON PRESS INC.

New York · Toronto · Oxford · Sydney

PERGAMON PRESS INC.
Maxwell House, Fairview Park, Elmsford, N.Y. 10523

PERGAMON OF CANADA LTD.
207 Queen's Quay West, Toronto 117, Ontario

PERGAMON PRESS LTD.
Headington Hill Hall, Oxford

PERGAMON PRESS (AUST.) PTY. LTD.
Rushcutters Bay, Sydney, N.S.W.

Third Printing

Printed in the United States of America
08 016823 X(H)
08 017061 7(S)

To Joan

Contents

Preface

This manual is designed for the nurse, teacher, or parent who is concerned with training or carrying out therapy with mentally retarded and autistic children in institutional or community settings. It is intended to be a comprehensive, practical "cook book" type of text that gives answers to the questions that are frequently asked by persons interested in training children with behavioral disorders. It was developed over a three-year period and has been standardized with approximately 500 speech therapists, teachers, nurses, psychiatric aides, attendants, and parents.

This manual has been written in everyday language. Principles have been deliberately kept to a minimum. They are discussed in simple, everyday terms, and are illustrated using experiences common to everyone. No attempt is made to teach the reader to talk like a psychologist. Instead, emphasis is placed on training the reader to become an effective behavior modifier who is capable of analyzing behavior disorders in children and modifying the child's behavior in the direction of normal behavior. Redundancy, which is annoying to some people, is used to facilitate learning the contents of the text.

This book evolved out of a Hospital Improvement Project grant and a Hospital Inservice Training Program grant awarded to the Columbus State Institute, Columbus, Ohio. In order to operate our Ward Behavior Modification Project, we needed a simply written, fairly straightforward text that could be understood by psychiatric aides and attendants. The manual was written for this purpose.

This book could never have been written without the support of certain crucial people. First, I would like to thank Miss Doris Haar and Dr.

Robert Jaslow of the Division of Mental Retardation, Social Rehabilitation Services, Health, Education, and Welfare, for providing financial support through three grants: the Hospital Improvement Grant (grant #51-P-70080-5-04), the Hospital Inservice Training Grant (grant #52-P-70174-5-04), and the Mental Retardation Facilities Community Staffing Grant (grant #5H01-MR-08181-02). I would also like to thank Dr. Roger Gove, Commissioner of Mental Retardation in Ohio for his support throughout these projects. I would like to express my thanks to Dr. Judith Rettig and Dr. Donald Lucas, former superintendents of Columbus State Institute and the current superintendent, Dr. Lloyd Covault, for their continued support. I would like to thank Miss Jan Brown, former Director of Nursing, and Mrs. Pat Amrine, current Director of Nursing at Columbus State Institute, for their cooperation and support on the HIP and HIST projects. In addition, I would like to thank all institutional behavior modification project staff for their energy and accomplishments over the past three years, particularly Mrs. Donna Brust, Mrs. Earnestine Johnson, and Mrs. Betty Borden. Our community project existed and succeeded as a result of the support and efforts of certain people. They were Dr. Bernard Niehm, Dr. Joan Bassinger, Mr. David Hoffman, Mr. Robert Young, and Mrs. Robin Blevins. To them I say thank you very much. Finally, I would like to thank Dr. Joan Bassinger, Mr. Christopher Sanders, and Mr. David Hoffman for editing the manual, and Mrs. Emma Bozymski, Mrs. Virginia Moore, Mrs. Judy Ore, and Mrs. Sharon Sieg for typing the manuscript.

LUKE WATSON

Introduction

This manual is designed to be read and understood by persons with little or no formal background in psychology or behavior modification. It is written specifically for persons who are involved in habilitating mentally retarded and autistic children: teachers, speech therapists, nurses, psychiatric aides, and parents. It is used as a training manual in our Columbus State Institute Behavior Modification Academic Program with a pre-recorded set of lectures that are presented in conjunction with 35 mm slides which illustrate the lecture material. There is also a set of test materials that allow the teacher to assess the trainee's understanding of the textbook and lecture material. When all of these materials are used together on a *contingent reinforcement* basis, the trainee benefits maximally. (This term is explained in the manual.) However, the manual can be used alone or in conjunction with a traditional lecture.

The reader is urged to progress through the text from the beginning to the end in the order the lectures are set up, as each lecture provides the basis for understanding each subsequent one. Periodically throughout the text the reader will find three types of "test" devices intended to help her assess and promote her understanding of the subject matter. The three types of test materials constitute a programming approach to developing certain concepts and principles considered by the author to be essential in understanding the subject matter. True-False tests and Fill-in the Blanks tests are designed to develop the kind of verbal behavior that will allow the reader to satisfactorily answer the Essay Questions and better understand the text.

If the manual is to be used to teach behavior modification, these same

T-F, fill-in and essay-type test materials can be used by an instructor to evaluate a student's classroom performance. It is the author's intention that the T-F and fill-in tests be used to assess understanding of the textbook, and the essay questions be used to evaluate the corresponding lecture given by the instructor.

Chapter 1 provides the reader with the rationale for using a behavior modification approach to training children. Psychopathology is viewed from the standpoint of being due to behavioral deficits or inappropriate behavior. Chapter 2 compares a behavioral approach to mental retardation and psychosis with more conventional medical and psychiatric approaches. Chapter 3 introduces three operant conditioning principles to the reader: reinforcement, shaping, and stimulus control. Chapters 4 and 5 consider the principle of shaping and its application to teaching children new behaviors. Chapters 6 and 7 deal with the principle of reinforcement, how it can be used to generate and maintain desirable behavior, and how reinforcement can be used effectively. Eliminating undesirable behavior is the subject matter of Chapter 8, and Chapter 9 is devoted to the importance of stimulus control for ensuring that children will behave appropriately. Finally, Chapter 10 describes and evaluates simple, easy to use charting or data collection procedures.

A series of carefully developed training programs also are available from Behavior Modification Technology, P.O. Box 23161 Columbus, Ohio, 43223. They enable the teacher, nurse, parent, psychologist, or administrator to carry out self-help skill, language, social-recreational, educational, and vocational training programs with relative ease. These programs are available in printed, videotape, and filmstrip form. They have been developed primarily with moderately, severely, and profoundly retarded children and with autistic children. In addition, an administrator's guide to setting up a behavior modification program and training staff also is available. All of these programs were designed to serve as supplements to this manual.

CHAPTER 1

What is Behavior Modification ?

Behavior modification is a discipline of psychotherapy. It is concerned primarily with changing behavior that is observed. The main point of interest is the *observable behavior* of the child. When a practitioner wants to identify a child's problem, he observes the child's behavior as opposed to looking at his IQ score or preoccupying himself with traditional diagnostic labels, like brain damage or autism or mongolism or phenylketonuria or other unobservable, underlying causes. He does this because he feels that it is the observable behavior of the child that most effectively will provide the key to his treatment.

As you progress through this book, you will continue to find references to the *child's behavior*. The notions of mental retardation or autism or learning disorder or emotional disturbance will be considered from a behavioral point of view. All treatment will also be discussed in terms of changing the child's observable behavior. The particular behavior modification technique presented in this book is the *Operant Conditioning* approach. Developed by Professor B. F. Skinner of Harvard University (Ferster and Skinner, 1957; and Skinner, 1953, 1957, 1968), it has proven to be a highly useful method for developing self-help, social-recreational, language, educational and vocational skills in mentally retarded, autistic, emotionally disturbed children and children with other learning disorders, both in institutions and in community settings (Bensberg, 1965; Browning and Stover, 1971; Bucher and Lovaas, 1966; Gardner, 1971; Lent, LeBlanc, and Spradlin, 1970; Patterson, 1971; Patterson and Gullion, 1968; and Watson, 1967).

1

THE RELEVANCE OF BEHAVIOR MODIFICATION TO YOU

What is the importance of the operant conditioning approach to behavior modification to you personally? What does it have to do with your daily way of life, particularly if you are a mother of an autistic or retarded child, a school teacher of such children, a nurse in an institution for the mentally retarded, a psychotherapist, or a student pursuing a special degree in a university? The answer is *everything*. Principles of operant conditioning dictate your behavior, the behavior of your fellow staff members, and the behavior of these children. The *Principle of Reinforcement* is a case in point. It states that the results of our actions or behavior determine whether or not we repeat that behavior. If you smile at someone (your behavior) and they do something nice for you in return (result), then you will probably smile more at people in the future (repeat behavior). If you drive through a red traffic light and receive a ticket, or are hit by a car, you will probably think twice before you run a red traffic light in the future and will do it less frequently. If you ask an "intelligent" question in class and your professor gives you special recognition for asking the question, you may be motivated to ask "intelligent" questions in class and find you are asking them more frequently in the future. If you fix your husband his favorite meal, spaghetti and meat balls with your special meat sauce, and he raves endlessly about how delicious it was, you will probably want to prepare him another special meal very soon, and you will enjoy preparing it more. Actually, the principle of reinforcement controls just about everything you do: the way you walk, the way you talk and how much you talk, the way you treat people and the way they treat you. In general, the principle of reinforcement states that if the results of behavior are positive, the behavior will likely be repeated. If the results of the behavior are negative, the behavior is less likely to recur. The principle of reinforcement determines what "stimuli" or cues will be important to you and what you will do or not do. All dimensions of our social life, our attitudes and/or our basic philosophy of life are controlled by the principle of reinforcement. Reinforcement also has the same effect on our friends, members of our community, and mentally retarded and autistic children as well. The principle of reinforcement accounts for the occurrence of a large part of the behavior that appears in children called mentally retarded or autistic or psychotic or brain damaged or emotionally disturbed, as will be described.

A second operant conditioning principle that dramatically emphasizes the word RELEVANCE for you is the *Principle of Stimulus Control*.

This principle states that certain cues or parts of your environment or the world you live in determine the things you do and when you will do them. A very simple example is a red traffic light. The light turns red as you approach it in your car and you stop. The red traffic light (a stimulus or cue) caused you to stop (behavior). The light turns green and you go. The green traffic light caused you to go. You see your lover or loved one approach you after an extended separation and you flush, your heart rate suddenly increases, you are overcome with an indescribable feeling of happiness, and you find yourself running to meet him. That is a stimulus control situation. He maintains this kind of stimulus control over your emotional and your locomotor behavior. You are repeating your graduate oral exam because you flunked it once before. You have to appear before the same group of three professors in the same conference room. As you approach the room for the exam you find you feel nauseated, your stomach is tied in knots, your mouth is dry and you cannot swallow; you cannot think of a thing to say as you walk into the room and you have an over-whelming impulse to run away. These are all examples of stimulus control. It permeates everything you do. It accounts for or controls almost all of your behavior, the behavior of your colleagues, and of children called autistic or emotionally disturbed or mentally retarded. All behavior is under stimulus control.

Principles of operant conditioning are relevant to you. They are relevant to all human beings, whether "normal" or otherwise. They are a fact of life. They constitute the laws of behavior. They can account for why there are good marriages or bad marriages; they can account for why people in a community live in harmony or whether they have demonstrations and riots over racial issues, campus disorders or equal rights for other minority groups. They also can account for why some children are good students in school and adjust well to their society or whether they have emo-tional/educational problems and become "neurotic" or "psychotic" or "criminals."

When applied accidentally, operant conditioning principles may contri-bute to the normal development of a child and his adjustment to the society in which he lives. However, accidental applications of these principles can also lead to abnormal adjustment, create problems for the child in school, result in emotional and/or behavior problems. When applied in a systematic, organized manner, they can contribute substan-tially to normal development and eliminate social-emotional-behavior problems. Persons who practice systematic application of operant con-ditioning principles to solve human behavior problems are engaging in behavior modification. Both professional and paraprofessional persons working under the supervision of professionals can use this method effectively to reduce the severity of behavioral disorders associated with mental retardation and autism. When they are applied systematically, operant conditioning principles can be used therapeutically to help solve a variety of human problems. Even if we are not aware of them, they still are operating all the time whenever two people are interacting with one another. *They are extremely relevant to all of us.*

This chapter deals with a behavioral interpretation of mental retardation and autism. The interpretation is both simple and practical. The particular point of view presented readily leads to a straightforward behavioristic treatment program. Both "retarded" and "autistic" children will be considered as if they belong to the same diagnostic class, since most children classified as "autistic" score mentally retarded on IQ tests and both "groups" display similar behaviors.

"ABNORMAL" BEHAVIOR

Society's Standards

People all have something in *common*, i.e., they are alike in many ways. They are also different from each other in certain ways. It is the things they have in common that become the standards of society. For example, people living in a town like Columbus, Ohio, have certain standards of conduct based on attitudes and activities or behavior they have in common. Some of these attitudes are a belief in God, belief that a man should have only one wife and should be married to a woman before he begins living with her, belief that a man should hold down a job and support his family, and belief that most laws should be obeyed. Some of these activities or behaviors are worshiping God in an established church, holding down a job, getting married and having babies, living in a house of a certain size and kind, wearing clothes of a certain general style, and driving a car, riding a bus or a taxi to go to work, to church, or to go to and from the grocery store where most of them obtain food. People who do these things are considered *"normal,"* *good*, and *moral* citizens because they are doing most of the things other people in Columbus like to do in a way most Columbus citizens like to do them. Again, these attitudes and activities which most people in Columbus hold in common constitute Columbus' *standards of conduct.*

These attitudes and activities or behaviors that people hold in common are not only the basis for society's standards, but also provide the source of the notion of *normality*. A person who behaves like the majority of other members of his community will be considered normal by his neighbors. If he wears the same kind of clothes, drives the same type of car, lives in a similar house, has a similar job, and has the same hobbies as his neighbors, they will classify him as normal. Such attitudes and behaviors are also the basis for a society's notions of *right* and *good* and *moral*.

*Circle a T or an F in Front of Each Statement**

T   F   (1) It is the things, attitudes, activities, or behaviors people in a community have in *common* that become society's *standards*.

T   F   (2) Society's standards are based on the *differences* between people – the difference in their attitudes, activities, or behaviors.

T   F   (3) Standards of conduct are based on attitudes, activities, and behaviors people in a community have in *common*.

T   F   (4) People who abide by society's *standards of conduct* are considered to be *normal, good*, and *moral* citizens.

T   F   (5) People who do *not* abide by society's standards of conduct are considered to be *normal* and *good* and *moral* citizens.

T   F   (6) The things that most people in a community like to do become the basis for that community's *standards* or *rules* of *appropriate conduct*.

T   F   (7) People in a community do *not* really care how members of their community act or behave.

Answers are on page 14.

Society's Prohibitions

However, all of the citizens of Columbus, Ohio, are different from each other in certain ways, and the extent to which they tolerate these behavioral differences in each other varies. All do not attend the same church. Some go to the Methodist church, others attend the Presbyterian church, while still others attend the Catholic church or a synagogue. All do not wear the same clothes. Some men wear conservative solid color suits, black or solid brown shoes, and rather plain ties. Others wear checked coats or pants, two-tone shoes, and ties that are brightly colored. Some drive Fords while others drive Buicks or Volkswagens. These are minor differences and little controversy is created among citizens by these differences.

Then there are other behavioral differences that will at least cause gossip among the citizenry. A person living in a neighborhood where houses are freshly painted and lawns and hedges neatly trimmed will cause a stir by not painting his house or by not mowing his lawn or trimming his hedge regularly; or a 45-year-old widow or divorcee who suddenly begins to date an 18-year-old man regularly will cause raised eyebrows; or a man who comes home drunk six nights a week and wakes the neighborhood by shouting obscenities at his wife will cause gossip and maybe even complaints to him from those living next door.

Then there are behavioral differences which the citizenry will not tolerate. A man who attacks a woman on the street and molests her sexually will probably be arrested; so will a man who robs a bank or a service station or kills another man. These differences are punishable by fines and imprisonment.

Autism and Mental Retardation

There are also still other behavioral differences that a community will not tolerate. These are, loosely speaking, acting too "crazy," or too "stupid." A person who hears voices that no one else hears and tells others about them may be placed in an institution. This will happen if he frightens someone, such as a member of the family or a neighbor and charges are pressed against him in a court of law. A child who is a constant behavior problem in school and his own neighborhood or acts and talks quite differently from other children in strange and bizarre ways may be diagnosed as emotionally disturbed or autistic. A child who is failing in school and makes an IQ score of 70 or less when tested will be labeled mentally retarded and probably placed in a special class. If he is also a severe behavior problem at home, his parents may have him committed to an institution for the mentally retarded; or if his parents die or abandon him, and the community authorities become responsible for him, he probably will be institutionalized.

Abnormality

It is these behavioral differences that make up a society's notion of *bad* or *wrong* or *abnormal*. An abnormal person is one who essentially behaves differently from others. The greater his behavioral differences, the more abnormal he will be considered. There also are special categories of behavior that are considered highly taboo such as committing rape or robbery, or believing you have a live snake in your belly, or being mute or uttering gibberish, or making an IQ score of 70 or less. These behaviors are placed in a special category, and laws have been passed about them.

These people are labeled criminal, crazy (psychotic), and mentally retarded.

In summary, society tolerates some behavioral differences in people more than others. Some may cause little more than gossip, while others can cause a person to be institutionalized. The main point of this comparison between behavioral likenesses and differences among people is to *emphasize* that *all people*, normal, crazy, and retarded, *have much in common. They are more alike* than they are different. Their differences may be few. Psychotic and retarded children are very much like you and me even though they are also different in other respects such as the way they walk, talk, and do certain things.

Circle a T or an F in Front of Each Statement*

T   F   (1) People in a community do *not* like other members of their community to behave *differently* from them.

T   F   (2) People in a community like other members of the community to act or behave *differently* from them.

T   F   (3) Members of a community may simply *gossip* about persons in their community who are not too different from them—if they are not too different.

T   F   (4) There are some behavioral differences which members of a community will not *tolerate* and are *punishable* by fines or imprisonment.

T   F   (5) Rape is an example of a behavioral *difference* that is punishable by *imprisonment*.

T   F   (6) Going to church on Friday night is an example of a behavioral *difference* that is punishable by *imprisonment*.

T   F   (7) Acting crazy or psychotic is an example of a behavioral *difference* that is punishable by institutionalization.

T   F   (8) Making an IQ score of 70 or less is an example of a behavioral difference that may cause a person to be institutionalized.

T   F   (9) All people—normal, crazy, criminal, or retarded—have much in *common*.

T   F   (10) People are more different from each other than they are alike.

T   F   (11) The *similarities* between people are greater than their *differences*, regardless of the nature of their differences.

T   F   (12) Mentally retarded and autistic children are more *like* normal people than they are *different*.

*Answers are on page 14.

Fill in the Missing Words*

(1) Society's *standards* are based on the attitudes, values and behaviors people in that society have in _____.

(2) People in a community like other members of the community to be _____ _____ them.
(3) Concepts of right, good, and moral are based on the attitudes, values, and behaviors members of that community have in _____.
(4) Society's _____ are based on the attitudes, values, and behaviors people in that society have in common.
(5) Members of a society do not _____ behavioral differences in other members of that society.
(6) Members of a society who are crazy, retarded, or criminal may be placed in _____.
(7) Retarded and autistic children behave _____ _____ normal children than they behave differently.

Answers are on page 14.

Answer These Questions*
(1) What are a society's standards based on?
(2) How do members of a society react to the differences in people?
(3) To what extent is a mentally retarded or autistic child like a normal child and to what extent does he differ from a normal child?

Answers are on pages 14–15.

HOW MENTALLY RETARDED AND AUTISTIC CHILDREN DIFFER FROM NORMAL CHILDREN

One of the criteria or *standards* for mental retardation is the level of intelligence. This is usually determined by standardized tests developed for that purpose. The score obtained on these tests is the Intelligence Quotient or IQ. Most children diagnosed as autistic also receive an IQ score that classifies them as mentally retarded. The lower the IQ level of the child, the more different he is behaviorally from "normal" persons. When I say he is different, I am talking about the way he acts — his *behavior*. Children with IQ scores from 51 to 70, known as the *Mildly Retarded*, may differ from "normal" children only in the way they talk (*see* Table 1.1). They may have a smaller vocabulary or be able to talk less about what is going on in the world or the things one learns about in school. They may pronounce their words just as well as you and I, but literally know less of them. In addition, they may not solve problems as well as you and I. If they miss their bus to work, they may be at a loss as to what they should do. They are lacking or are deficient in *verbal behavior*. But in other respects they may be pretty much like "normal" people. Children with IQ's from 36 to 50, called *Moderately Retarded*, not only have less language, but also may talk "funny" (unclearly), walk awkwardly, and behave differently in other ways. They may have coordination problems which make them awkward or clumsy. They may wear their clothes in a way that makes them look bizarre, and they will lack a number of other behaviors such as athletic skills. Children with IQ's from 35 to 0, the

Table 1.1   Class of Mental Retardate, IQ Level and General Behavioral Characteristics.

Class	IQ Range	Behavioral Characteristics As compared with normal persons
Mildly	51–70	(1) Says fewer words (2) Solves some problems with difficulty
Moderately	36–50	(1) Says even fewer words (2) Has difficulty solving simple everyday problems (3) Poorly coordinated (4) Sloppy dress (5) Lacks work skills
Severely	20–35	(1) Says very few words (2) Does not solve simple everyday problems (3) Poorly coordinated (4) Numerous physical defects (5) Does not dress self and usually not toilet trained
Profoundly	19 or less	(1) Says very few words or none (2) Does not solve simple everyday problems (3) Poorly coordinated (4) Numerous physical defects (5) Does not dress self and usually not toilet trained (6) Requires almost total nursing care (7) Does not feed self with utensils

Severely and *Profoundly Retarded*, are the most different behaviorally. They eat differently, walk differently, usually do not talk, often are not toilet trained, and behave in a variety of very strange ways. All of these children are different from normal children in two basic ways: *they have less behavior and the behavior they exhibit is socially inappropriate.*

Less Behavior

How can we account for these differences in behavior between the "normal" and retarded or autistic child? One reason is because retarded and autistic children literally have *less behavior* than normal children. Perhaps an analogy will help to clarify the point. Imagine a bucket that represents the variety, amount or number of behaviors a normal child has (*see* Fig. 1.1). When the bucket is filled to the brim it represents the total variety, amount or number of behaviors the average normal child of a given age possesses. Proceeding with this analogy, the mildly retarded child is very much like the normal child except that he has less language and his judgment is not as good. So we see his behavior level is slightly lower in the bucket than the normal child. When we go to the moderately retarded child, we find he not only has less language and poorer judgment as compared with the normal child, but is also quite clumsy or poorly coordinated. Because of his poor coordination he lacks quite a number of behaviors that the normal child has and his behavioral level is still lower in the bucket. When we get down to the severely and profoundly retarded, they have such a small number and such a limited variety of behaviors that they fill only the lower half of the bucket. Thus, the severely and profoundly retarded are *most deficient* in behavior when compared with the normal child, and the *profoundly retarded child is most deficient of all.*

Inappropriate Behavior

In addition to having less behavior than the normal child, there is one other reason that the mentally retarded or autistic child is different behaviorally from normal children. Much of the behavior he has occurs *inappropriately.* Let us use the profoundly retarded child as an example of this factor. He can eat but he may eat sticks, string, and feces as well as food, or he eats with his fingers instead of using a spoon or a fork. Eating is a behavior common to both normal and retarded children, but the behavior occurs inappropriately, i.e., eating sticks, string, or feces, or food with his fingers rather than with a spoon. A second example is elimination, i.e., defecation and urination. The profoundly retarded child usually urinates or defecates in his pants or on the floor rather than in the toilet. Elimination is a behavior common to both normal and retarded persons, but elimination on the floor or in one's pants rather than in the toilet is inappropriate.

Another example is seeking attention. Everyone wants attention from other people and there are appropriate and inappropriate ways to get it.

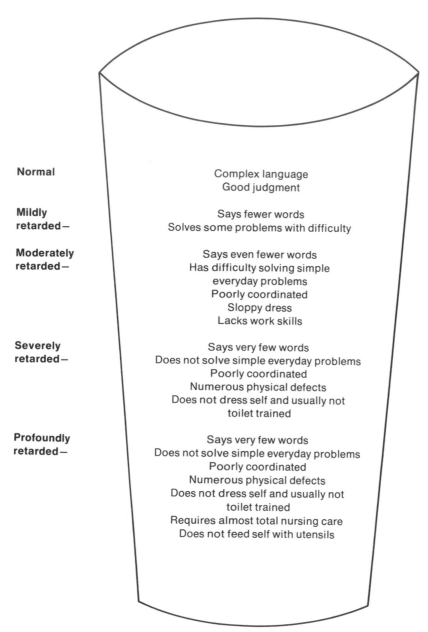

Fig. 1.1 Diagram of "Behavioral Bucket." This bucket contains different kinds and amounts of behaviors.

Calling someone by name politely is an appropriate way to get attention. Beating your head against walls is an inappropriate way to get attention. Profoundly retarded children often do this to get attention. It is the inappropriate aspects of their behavior that make autistic, severely and profoundly retarded children appear to be strange or crazy.

Inappropriate behavior occurs for two reasons. The person may have behavior which would be appropriate in a particular situation but does not use it, or he may not have the behavior that would be appropriate for that situation at all. Let us use elimination as an example. A child may know how to use the toilet, but may defecate or urinate in his pants anyway. In other words, he may have the proper elimination behavior, but still not use it appropriately. Or he may simply not know how to use the toilet and may soil or wet himself; he is lacking in toileting behavior. We have a child at Columbus State Institute who soiled himself daily. One day we introduced a new type of training pants to the ward as part of a new toilet training program. We told him not to "mess in his pretty new pants." He did not. He used the toilet daily from that point on throughout the toilet training program. He evidently had toileting behavior in his behavioral repertoire, but did not use it. Once he started getting attention for using the toilet and not soiling his pants, he started using it. Then there are other children who have to be taught behaviors related to using the toilet: from sitting on it with their pants down, to walking to it from another part of the house or building when they have to defecate or urinate. They appear to have little or no toileting behavior at all.

SUMMARY

From a behavioral point of view, mentally retarded and autistic children are different from normal children for two basic reasons. First, they have *less* behavior in their behavioral repertoires, and second, much of the behavior they have occurs *inappropriately*.

*Circle a T or F in Front of Each Statement**

T   F   (1) The lower the IQ level of the child, the more *different* he is behaviorally from normal children.

T   F   (2) Mildly retarded children are behaviorally more *like* normal children than severely retarded children.

T   F   (3) Moderately retarded children are behaviorally more *different* from normal children than are profoundly retarded children.

T   F   (4) Profoundly retarded children are behaviorally more *different* from normal children than mildly, moderately, or severely retarded children.

T   F   (5) Mentally retarded children are *different* from normal children in two ways: they have *less* behavior and their behavior occurs *inappropriately*.

T   F   (6) Mentally retarded children are *different* from normal children in two ways: they have *less* behavior and they are *stupid*.

T   F   (7) Mentally retarded children are *different* from normal people in two ways: they are *stupid* and they are *lazy*.

T   F   (8) Mentally retarded children are *different* from normal children in two ways: they are *lazy* and their behavior occurs *inappropriately*.

Answers are on page 15.

Fill in the Missing Words*

(1) The lower the IQ level of the child, the more _____ he is behaviorally from the normal child.

(2) The mildly retarded child is more _____ normal children than the severely retarded child.

(3) The profoundly retarded child is more _____ from normal children than the moderately retarded child.

(4) The _____ retarded child is more *different* from normal children than the other three classes of retardates.

(5) The _____ retarded child is more *like* normal children than the other three classes of retardates.

(6) Retarded and autistic children differ from normal children in two ways: they have _____ behavior and their behavior occurs _____ .

Answers are on page 15.

Answer These Questions*

(1) How does the *mildly retarded* child differ from a normal child?

(2) How does the *moderately retarded* child differ from a normal child?

(3) How does the *severely retarded* child differ from a normal child?

(4) How does the *profoundly retarded* child differ from a normal child?

(5) Which one of these four kinds of retardates is most different from a normal child?

(6) What are the two ways that retarded and autistic children differ behaviorally from normal children?

Answers are on page 15.

Answers to T-F, Fill-in, and Essay Questions

T-F on page 5
- (1) T
- (2) F
- (3) T
- (4) T
- (5) F
- (6) T
- (7) F

T-F on page 7
- (1) T
- (2) F
- (3) T
- (4) T
- (5) T
- (6) F
- (7) T
- (8) T
- (9) T
- (10) F
- (11) T
- (12) T

Fill-in on pages 7–8
- (1) common
- (2) like
- (3) common
- (4) standards
- (5) tolerate or permit
- (6) prisons or institutions
- (7) more like

Essay Questions on page 8
- (1) Society's standards are based on the attitudes, values, and behaviors that people in that society have in common.

(2)   Members of a society react to differences in people in that society by gossiping about them, leaving them alone, and imprisoning them.
(3)   The mentally retarded and autistic child is more like a normal child than he is different.

T-F on pages 12–13
   (1)   T
   (2)   T
   (3)   F
   (4)   T
   (5)   T
   (6)   F
   (7)   F
   (8)   F

Fill-in on page 13
   (1)   different
   (2)   like
   (3)   different
   (4)   profoundly
   (5)   mildly
   (6)   less; inappropriately

Essay Questions on page 13
   (1)   The mildly retarded child says fewer words and solves some problems with difficulty.
   (2)   The moderately retarded child says even fewer words than the mildly retarded child, has difficulty solving simple everyday problems, is poorly coordinated, dresses sloppily, and lacks work skills.
   (3)   The severely retarded child says very few words, does not solve simple everyday problems, is poorly coordinated, has numerous physical defects, usually does not dress himself, and usually is not toilet trained.
   (4)   The profoundly retarded child says a few words or none at all, does not solve simple everyday problems, is poorly coordinated, has numerous physical defects, does not dress himself, is usually not toilet trained, requires almost total nursing care, and usually does not feed himself with utensils.
   (5)   The profoundly retarded child is most different from a normal child.
   (6)   They have *less behavior* and the behavior they do have is *socially inappropriate*.

CHAPTER 2

Psychoeducational Treatment of Autism, Mental Retardation, and Behavioral Disorders

In the previous chapter, mental retardation and autism were considered to be very similar, from a behavioral point of view. Both were described as disorders resulting from two behavioral deficiencies: (1) such children have *less behavior* than "normal" children of the same age, and (2) much of their behavior is *socially inappropriate*. This is a *behavioral* interpretation which says nothing about underlying anatomical or biochemical *causes* of these disorders resulting from disease or physical injury.

Briefly, let us examine the basis for this neglect, i.e., ignoring causes of these disorders. First, in the majority of cases labeled "mentally retarded" and those called "autistic," the causes of these disorders are unknown. Secondly, in those cases of mental retardation for which a cause (etiology) has been identified, the relationship between the "causal agent" and the resulting mental retardation (behavioral disorder) is almost always unknown. For example, mongolism (Down's Syndrome) is said to be the result of a chromosomal disorder. However, it is still not clear what caused the chromosomal abnormality or why several different types of abnormalities in chromosomes result in the same syndrome of mongolism. In addition, the relationship between the syndrome and the behavior such a child exhibits is still not known. Another example is measles. A number of persons contract measles every year, and, except for some discomfort experienced when they have the disease, many do not have serious aftereffects. In a small number of cases, however, encephalitis and mental retardation results from measles. As to why this occurs, we do not have an answer. Again, the relationship between the disorder and the behavior produced is not known.

A third reason for ignoring the cause of mental retardation and autism is related to treatment. Since we do not know the cause in the majority of cases, medically speaking, we do not know how or what to treat. In those cases where we can specify a cause, we do not have the means to eliminate the damage that has occurred to the nervous system of the child (the cause of the "mental disorder") once it occurs.

Since identification of the *medical cause* of the mentally retarded or autistic child's disorder currently contributes very little to our ability to eliminate the child's level of retardation or psychosis, the traditional medical diagnosis presently is of little value to the person interested in habilitating these children, once the damage has occurred. However, we do know that regardless of the origin of the damage to the child, he can benefit from education, particularly if the educational program is designed for a specific child with a specific behavioral disorder. It should be emphasized that although behavior modification deemphasizes the importance of underlying causes of mental retardation and autism, and emphasizes the observable behavior, this does not imply that advocates of behavior modification are not aware that continued research as to cause and effect of mental retardation and autism should be continued. They are indeed conscious that at some future date, increased knowledge of the relationship between biochemical and anatomical disorders of the nervous system and behavioral disorders may play an important role in treatment of mentally retarded and autistic children.

Psychological factors can contribute to all mental retardation or behavioral disorders or help to increase the severity of them, regardless of their initial cause. Some of the behavior exhibited by these children is learned to some extent. Once children are diagnosed as autistic or mentally retarded, their opportunities to benefit from the usual educational experiences are reduced (a lack of opportunity to learn). This can occur for two reasons. First, once parents learn their child is retarded or autistic, they may become discouraged and not provide him with the same learning opportunities they do for their normal children. If the child is institutionalized, his opportunities to learn normal behavior usually will be dramatically reduced because of lack of staff to interact with him, and because of the tendency of many institutional staff to inadvertently promote psychotic and retarded behavior. It appears that staff in residential institutions and parents may even accidentally teach children to act retarded or autistic. This is not done deliberately, of course. It often happens because such people are trying to cope with these children and are not aware of the influence of the way they deal with them. Secondly, since many of these children are either negativistic or apathetic, many mothers, teachers, and residential institutional staff who attempt to educate them become discouraged and give up, i.e., they stop trying to teach them. However, *no matter what the cause of the disorder, the behavior of every child can be improved through education or training*, but the educational procedure must be designed for the specific child with a specific behavioral disorder.

*Circle a T or F in Front of Each Statement**

T   F   (1) It is important to determine the medical cause of mental retardation or autism before planning a behavior modification program for a child.

T   F   (2) It is not important to attempt to determine the medical cause of behavioral disorders when preparing to train a child, since in many cases of mental retardation and autism, the cause is unknown.

T   F   (3) Regardless of the original cause, all retardates or children with behavior disorders can benefit from psychoeducational treatment.

T   F   (4) Only persons who became mentally retarded or have behavior disorders due to environmental reasons can benefit from psychoeducational treatment.

Answers are on page 21.

PSYCHOEDUCATIONAL TREATMENT

Much of the behavior that identifies a child as being mentally retarded or autistic is exhibited by normal children. The difference is that such behavior is not seen as frequently in normal children or it is not seen under such unusual circumstances. Thus, most abnormal behavior is classified as such because it occurs more frequently than it does in the "normal" child or because it occurs under highly unusual social circumstances. For example, every child occasionally rocks or cries or slaps his head and no one thinks much of it. But, if he spends most of the day rocking (without the aid of a rocking chair), crying or slapping himself repeatedly in the face, people become concerned, particularly if he exhibits very little other behavior. If this kind of behavior continues over a long period of time, the child may be labeled psychotic or emotionally disturbed. Or if the child uses temper tantrums excessively to control his parents and teachers, i.e., get them to do what he wants them to do, or if he slaps himself in the face to communicate he wants to be held and caressed by his mother, he may well be diagnosed psychotic. Finally, another behavioral characteristic that epitomizes the mentally retarded or autistic child is that he does not exhibit certain behaviors usually found in children identified as "normal." He may not talk or he may not hug or kiss his parents or sit in their laps, or he may neither undress nor dress himself even though he is eight years old.

As previously indicated, from a behavioral point of view, the autistic and/or retarded child appears to be different from normal children for two reasons: first, he lacks behavior usually found in normal children; and second, much of the behavior he exhibits occurs under socially inappropriate circumstances. Any effective behavior modification habilitation program must deal with those two problems. If the child is to be habilitated: (1) *he must be taught more behavior to eliminate his problem of having less behavior*, and (2) *he must be taught to exhibit behavior under socially appropriate circumstances, to eliminate his inappropriate behavior problem.* Thus, not only should he be taught to take off his clothing, but he also should be taught when and where to remove his clothing — not in the living room, or the classroom or the lunch room or the playground, but rather, in the bathroom at toileting time, or the bedroom at clothes changing or dressing time or at bedtime. The same would be true for language. Not only should he be taught to speak, but he also should be taught when and where to say certain words or phrases.

The goal of behaviorally oriented psychoeducational treatment is to *increase the child's behavioral repertoire* and to *get all behavior to occur appropriately.* The operant conditioning type of behavior modification is ideally suited for training autistic and mentally retarded children. It seems to be admirably suited for these children for six reasons:

1. It motivates the apathetic or negativistic child to learn.
2. It provides techniques for eliminating undesirable behavior, such as head slapping and temper tantrums.
3. It does not require that the child have language skills — it can be used effectively with mutes.
4. It does not require a minimal educational or experiential repertoire — it can be used even with the profoundly mentally retarded or profoundly autistic child.
5. It vastly simplifies the educational process by means of the *shaping* procedure.
6. Training progresses at the child's own pace.

Some of the more conventional psychoeducational procedures may be effective for dealing with the mildly and borderline retarded and even the moderately mentally retarded or brain damaged children who are not too negativistic. But severely and profoundly retarded children or highly negativistic children (such as the autistic child) will probably require more specialized procedures that are better suited for their particular type of problem. For additional points of view about the problem of psychopathology *see* Bijou (1966), Ferster (1961, 1965), Szasz (1969), and Ullmann and Krasner (1965).

Circle a T or F in Front of Each Statement*

T   F   (1) The objective of psychoeducational treatment of mentally retarded and autistic children is to increase their behavioral repertoires and to get all behavior to occur appropriately.

T   F   (2) The operant conditioning method is admirably suited for training these children because it neither requires that they have language skills nor other specific behavioral skills. In addition, it provides techniques for motivating the child and eliminating undesirable behavior.

*Answers are on page 21.

Fill in the Missing Words*

(1) It usually is not useful to know the medical _____ of a behavioral disorder when placing a child in a psychoeducational treatment program.

(2) Regardless of the original cause of the disorder, all children can benefit from _____ treatment.

(3) The objective of psychoeducational treatment of mentally retarded and autistic children is to increase their _____ _____ _____ and to get all behavior to occur _____.

*Answers are on page 21.

Answer These Questions*

(1) Why is it not important to know the medical cause of behavioral disorders?

(2) What does psychoeducational treatment do to the behavior of such a child?

*Answers are on page 21.

Answers to T-F, Fill-in, and Essay Questions

T-F on page 18
- (1)   F
- (2)   T
- (3)   T
- (4)   F

T-F on page 20
- (1)   T
- (2)   T

Fill-in on page 20
- (1)   cause or diagnosis
- (2)   psychoeducational
- (3)   behavioral repertoires; appropriately

Essay Questions on page 20
- (1)   It is not important to know the medical cause of behavioral disorders because:
  - (a) in the majority of cases of mental retardation and autism, the cause is unknown;
  - (b) in the majority of cases where the cause is known, it is not clear how the causal agent produced the behavioral disorder;
  - (c) in the majority of cases, we do not know the medical cause and therefore do not know what to treat.
- (2)   Psychoeducational treatment increases the child's behavioral repertoire and gets it to occur under socially appropriate circumstances.

CHAPTER 3

The Operant Conditioning Method

The *operant conditioning method* is primarily concerned with developing voluntary behavior in people. This is behavior directly controlled by the child, such as walking, talking, drinking a glass of water, or riding a bicycle. This is in contrast to reflexive behavior which is not directly controlled by the child such as salivation, heartbeat, digestion, or sneezing. The term *operant* refers to behavior under the child's voluntary control. It is called *operant behavior* because it operates on the environment to provide the child with reinforcement or rewards, such as food, water, money, warmth, entertainment, etc. The operant "turning on the water tap" provides the child with water which he can use to fill a glass. The operant "lifting a glass of water to one's lips" provides the child even more directly with water in the mouth which can then be swallowed and thus quench one's thirst. The act of swallowing is also an operant; or the entire process of turning on a water tap, filling a glass, lifting it to one's lips, filling the mouth, and swallowing can be considered to be an operant which could simply be called "getting a drink of water."

*Circle a T or an F in Front of Each Statement**

T   F   (1) The *operant conditioning method* is primarily concerned with developing *voluntary* behavior in children, behavior directly controlled by the child himself — such as walking, talking, drinking a glass of water, or riding a tricycle.

T   F   (2) The *operant conditioning method* is primarily concerned with developing *reflexive* behavior in children, behavior not directly controlled by the child — such as heartbeat, breathing, digestion, and eyeblink.

T   F   (3) *Operant behavior* is behavior that operates on the *environment* to provide a child with reinforcements or rewards — such as food, water, money, warmth, entertainment, etc.

Answers are on page 37.

REINFORCEMENT

The operant conditioning method uses a principle of *reinforcement* as its main concept. The term reinforcement refers to a reward that a child likes such as money, attention, food, being caressed, or *something that he will expend some effort to obtain*. The basic premise is that *all behavior occurs because it provides the child with reinforcement*. In other words, learning occurs only when the child receives reinforcement for some behavior, and conversely, does not occur when no reinforcement is forthcoming. A child learns his ABC's because he gets some kind of self-satisfaction or attention from others for saying them. The baby learns to say "ma-ma" because saying "ma-ma" provides him with a big smile, a hug and words of praise from mother. The child learns to say, "May I please have a cookie," because mother gives him one when he says it. The child learns to say, "I love you, Mother," because saying it gets him a smile, a word of affection, and maybe a hug from mother, and may also provide a feeling of satisfaction within the child.

There is a large variety of available reinforcements. Food is a powerful reinforcement for most children, particularly meals. Such food items as pretzels, corn chips, potato chips, crackers, candy, ice cream, and the numerous dry, presweetened breakfast cereals are preferred by most children. Children are also fond of things to drink, such as milk, water, Koolade, coffee, fruit juice, cola, and other carbonated beverages. However, all children do not like things to eat or drink between meals. They may prefer small toys to play with, such as a ball, a toy truck, or a music box toy. Others prefer to play with larger toys, e.g., a tricycle, a wagon, or a Krazy Kar. Still others prefer attention or affection from a favorite adult or friend. It is important to remember that all children do not like the same things as reinforcements. For this reason it is necessary to identify individual reinforcement preferences for each child when he is started in a training program.

Contingent Reinforcement

It is not simply the act of giving the reinforcement that accounts for learning occurring. It is the occurrence of reinforcement *because the child did something to get it* that is the crucial factor that makes behavior occur. The child learns to say, "May I please have a cookie," because his mother required him to say it in order that he get the cookie which is the reinforcement. The contingency or requirement for getting the cookie was saying, "May I please have a cookie." When someone is required to do something to get a reinforcement, this requirement is called a *reinforcement contingency*. The effect of the reinforcement is to strengthen and increase the occurrence of the behavior that just preceded it.

The following is an example of the use of contingent reinforcement to obtain desirable behavior. A boy rudely demands of his father, "Gimme some potato chips!" The father does not like this type of behavior and therefore does not reinforce and strengthen it by giving his son potato chips. Instead, he says, "Young man, if you want potato chips you will have to say politely, 'Please, may I have potato chips.'" At this point, the father gives them to him and adds, "That's better." The contingency the boy had to satisfy to get the potato chips was to ask for them politely. The reinforcement he received was the potato chips.

In a second example, a resident asks for permission to leave the ward for lunch. Since the rule is that only residents wearing bibs can go to lunch and the child is not wearing a bib, the nurse says, "No, not until you put on your bib," and she hands the resident a bib. The resident puts on the bib, and the nurse then lets him go to the dining hall for lunch. The contingency that the resident had to satisfy to get to lunch was to put on the bib. The reinforcement he received for putting on the bib was to be allowed to go to lunch.

The reinforcement contingency technique is the most powerful single tool in the behavior modification system. When used judiciously and properly, it will solve most of the problems in most behavior management situations. It is to the reader's advantage to learn to use it well.

Conclusion

This principle of reinforcement is the most important principle you will encounter in this manual. It motivates or energizes the non-motivated (apathetic) or negatively motivated (negativistic) child to begin to work or train where he formerly did nothing or even created a disturbance during training sessions. It also serves to provide the child with feedback. It lets him know he is performing correctly in the training situation. However, in order for reinforcement to be effective in a training situation, it must be strong enough or powerful enough to motivate the child or to make him work. More will be said about this problem in Chapter 6.

*Circle a T or an F in Front of Each Statement**

T   F   (1) Reinforcement is something like a *reward*, something a child *likes*.
T   F   (2) Learning occurs because the child gets some kind of reinforcement.
T   F   (3) Learning occurs whether the child gets reinforcement or does not get reinforcement. It is not important to use reinforcement when training children.
T   F   (4) The crucial factor that makes reinforcement important for training is that the child is required to do something to get the reinforcement.
T   F   (5) A contingency is the requirement or thing a child has to do to get a reinforcement.
T   F   (6) When someone is required to do something to get a reinforcement, this requirement is called a *reinforcement contingency*.
T   F   (7) In order for a reinforcement to be effective in a training situation, it must be powerful enough to get the child to work.

Answers are on page 37.

SHAPING

A contingent reinforcement procedure is a powerful training tool. We can use this technique to teach *new behavior* to severely retarded or psychotic children. However, this procedure alone is insufficient for teaching new behavior to such children. We need an additional technique if we are to provide them with a number of complex behavioral skills. We need a teaching method that is suitable for children with little or no language skills and very limited behavioral repertoires or experience. Such a method is the *shaping* technique. Shaping literally refers to molding simple behavior into more complex behavior of different kinds. This technique can be used to teach children toileting skills, dressing skills, language skills, social-recreational skills, educational skills, and vocational skills. The shaping technique is made up of two procedures: *successive approximation* and *chaining*. The successive approximation procedure is used to teach a single piece of behavior, such as eliminating in the toilet, taking off a pullover shirt, or putting on pants. The chaining procedure is used to string or connect a series of pieces of behavior together, e.g., in a dressing situation where the child puts on his underpants, pants, shirt, socks, and shoes in one continuous sequence.

Successive Approximation

Let us consider successive approximation first. How would we take a complex behavior like eliminating in the toilet and teach it to a child

using the successive approximation procedure? We would first analyze this behavior into small components, small enough to be readily learned by a profoundly retarded or severely autistic child, and teach them to him one small step at a time. For example, toileting behavior can be broken down into seven steps:

1. sitting,
2. eliminating,
3. taking down pants,
4. pulling up pants,
5. gaining independence from the trainer,
6. opening the bathroom door and walking to the toilet unescorted, and then returning to the bathroom door when the toileting act is completed,
7. walking to the bathroom door unescorted from another room in the ward, school, or home, and returning when the toileting act is completed.

The child would first be taught only to sit for a period of time ranging from approximately 3–5 minutes. Some children will only sit for a few seconds initially. So the child might be reinforced for sitting 5 seconds at first. Then she would gradually be required to sit longer and longer for reinforcement, perhaps 6 seconds, then 8, then 10, then 12, 20, 25, 30, 40, 50, 60, 80, 100, 120, 150, 180, 210, 250, 270, and 300 seconds or 5 minutes. Once she was sitting reliably, she would be placed on the toilet at the time she ordinarily eliminated. Then when she eliminated, she would be reinforced. The trainer would say, "Good girl," with a big smile and a lot of enthusiasm, give her some candy or Koolade and a pat on the back. Next, the child would be taught to take down her panties before she sat on the toilet and eliminated for reinforcement. She would next be required to pull up her panties after she got up from the toilet following elimination. At this point, the trainer would teach the child to be less dependent on her for carrying out the eliminative act. The trainer would gradually physically withdraw from the toilet area until the child was eliminating in the toilet with no one else present in the bathroom. Then the child would learn to open the bathroom door, walk over to the toilet, take down her panties, sit down on the toilet seat, eliminate, get up, pull up her panties, walk over to the bathroom door, open it, and walk out of the bathroom.

Next, she would be taught to walk to the bathroom from another part of the ward or school or house, open the bathroom door, walk over to the toilet, take down her panties, sit on the toilet, eliminate, get up, pull up her panties, walk over to the bathroom door, open it, and go back to the room which she had left to go to the toilet. At this point, the child is toilet scheduled, i.e., she will go to the toilet when told to by someone but does not independently go on her own. The final step in training is to teach her to respond independently to her own bowel and bladder cues without being reminded or cued by someone else. This can be accomplished by waiting until elimination is about to occur or is beginning to occur and telling the child to go to the toilet. Many children indicate that they are about to eliminate by going into an "eliminative posture" or making grunting sounds. A child who is told "No! Go to the toilet," when she is in the act of urinating may become more aware of her own bowel and bladder cues, anticipate elimination, and walk to the toilet and eliminate there.

A second example of using the successive approximation procedure is teaching a child to take off a short-sleeved pullover shirt (Fig. 3.1). The child is taught in a backward fashion, one small step at a time, and training always progresses at his own pace. The child is first taught to grasp the garment (Fig. 3.1-1). When this is done, the child is given reinforcement. Some of these children initially will not grasp clothing when told to do so. Then, he would be taught only one additional small step in taking off his shirt. He would be taught to take the shirt off the wrist of one hand, and be reinforced when the shirt cleared his hand (Fig. 3.1-2). Then, he would be taught to remove the shirt from around his elbow, and he would be reinforced again when the shirt cleared his hand (Fig. 3.1-3). The next step would be to teach him to remove the shirt from his shoulder, then the left arm, and he would be reinforced when the shirt cleared his left hand (Fig. 3.1-4). Then, he would be taught to remove the shirt from his head, followed by taking it off his left arm, and he would be reinforced when the shirt cleared his left hand (Fig. 3.1-5). Next, he would be required to take his right arm out of the right sleeve of the shirt, pull it off his head, take it off his left arm, and he would receive his reinforcement when the shirt cleared his left hand (Fig. 3.1-6). Next, he would be required to take the hem of the shirt, which would be positioned just below his nipples, pull the hem of the shirt up as high as he could, remove the right arm from the right sleeve of the shirt, pull the shirt off his head, take it off his left arm, and he would receive his reinforcement when the shirt cleared his left hand (Fig. 3.1-7). Finally, the hem of the shirt would be in the normal waist position (Fig. 3.1-8). The child would lift up the hem of the shirt as high as he could (Fig. 3.1-7), remove his right arm from the right sleeve (Fig. 3.1-6), pull the shirt off his head (Fig. 3.1-5), take the shirt off his left arm (Fig. 3.1-4), and he would be reinforced when the shirt cleared his

Fig. 3.1-1   The child is taught to grasp the garment.

Fig. 3.1-2   The child is taught to take the shirt off the left wrist.

Fig. 3.1-3   The child is taught to remove the shirt from the left elbow.

Fig. 3.1-4   The child is taught to remove the shirt from his left shoulder.

Fig. 3.1-5   The child is taught to remove the shirt from his head.

Fig. 3.1-6   The child is taught to remove the shirt from his right arm.

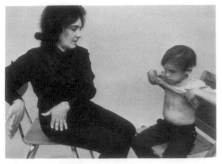

Fig. 3.1-7   The child is taught to remove the shirt from just below his nipples.

Fig. 3.1-8   The child is taught to remove the shirt from his waist.

left hand. The child always has to complete the undressing act before he gets reinforced. Reinforcement is always given at the same point — when the shirt is removed from the left hand.

A third example of successive approximation is taking off pants. Using the last step first, backward training procedure, the child is first taught to remove his pants from only one ankle and is reinforced at the point where the pants fall from his left foot. Next, he is taught to take the pants off of both ankles, removing the pants from the right ankle first followed by removing them from the left ankle, and he is reinforced when the pants fall from his left foot. Then he is taught to push the pants down from his calves, take them off the right foot, then the left foot, and he is reinforced. He is next taught to push the pants down from his knees, down to his ankles, remove the pants from his right foot, then from his left foot, and he is reinforced. Next, he is taught to push the pants down from his mid-thighs, down to his ankles, remove the pants from his right foot, then his left foot, and he is reinforced. He is then taught to take his pants down from his crotch, push them down to his ankles, remove the pants from his right foot, then his left foot, and he is reinforced. Finally, the child is taught to take his pants down from his normal waist position, push them down to his ankles, remove the pants from his right foot, then his left foot, and he is reinforced. Moving from one step to the next in training proceeds at the child's own pace. You move to each new step after he appears to have mastered the previous step. If he is rushed through the training, he will become confused and appear to forget what he has already learned. The size of the training steps will depend upon the child. Children who learn slowly or with difficulty require smaller or more steps than those who learn faster.

Chaining

Once a set of individual pieces of behavior have been taught separately to a child using the successive approximation procedure, e.g., putting on underpants, putting on pants, putting on shirt, putting on socks, and putting on shoes, we usually want to connect all of these behaviors together in one continuous behavioral sequence, such as dressing (Fig. 3.2). Connecting all of these behaviors together in a smooth sequence requires the chaining procedure. Just as in the successive approximation situation, individual units of behavior are taught in a backward fashion with the child being reinforced after the last unit is completed. We would begin by having the child completely dressed except for his shoes. Then we would say, "Freddy, get dressed," and reinforce him after he had put on both shoes (Fig. 3.2-1). We would begin the next training session with the child dressed except for socks and shoes (Fig. 3.2-2). He would be required to put on his socks and then his shoes for reinforcement. During the next training session, the child would already have on his pants and underpants (Fig. 3.2-3), and he would be required to put on his shirt followed by his socks followed by his shoes for reinforcement. Next, the child would have on his underpants (Fig. 3.2-4), and he would be required to put on his pants, then his shirt, then his socks, and then his shoes, and he would be reinforced after both shoes were on. Finally, the child would be nude and would be required to put on his underpants, followed by putting on his pants, followed by putting on his shirt, followed by putting on his socks, followed by putting on his shoes, and he would be reinforced when both shoes were on. Each piece or unit of behavior can be thought of as a link in the dressing chain, hence the name *chaining*.

Conclusion

In conclusion, the shaping technique consists of two procedures: successive approximation and chaining. Individual pieces or units of behavior are taught using a successive approximation procedure. Once the individual units are taught, they are connected together sequentially by means of the chaining procedure. When the *shaping* procedure is used to get behavior to occur a step at a time, and *reinforcement* is given when the behavior does occur, one has a very useful method for teaching a child a *new behavior*.

*Circle a T or an F in Front of Each Statement**
T   F   (1) Shaping refers to molding a figure of moist clay.
T   F   (2) Shaping is a technique used to mold simple behavior into more complex behavior.

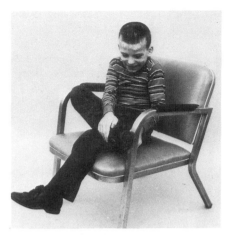

Fig. 3.2-1   The child puts on his shoes.

Fig. 3.2-2   The child puts on his socks.

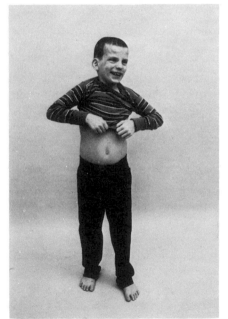

Fig. 3.2-3   The child puts on his shirt.

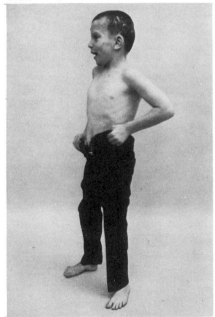

Fig. 3.2-4   The child puts on his pants.

T   F   (3) The shaping technique is made up of two other procedures: successive approximation and chaining.

T   F   (4) The successive approximation technique is made up of two other procedures: shaping and chaining.

T F (5) The successive approximation procedure is used to teach a single unit or piece of behavior, like putting on a shirt or a pair of pants.

T F (6) The successive approximation procedure is used to teach a complex behavioral sequence, like dressing.

T F (7) The chaining procedure is used to teach a complex behavioral sequence, like dressing.

T F (8) A shaping-reinforcement procedure is used to teach a retardate *more* or *new* behavior.

T F (9) A shaping-reinforcement procedure is used to get behavior to occur appropriately.

Answers are on page 37.

STIMULUS CONTROL

As pointed out in the section on causes of mental retardation and autism, such children are not only behaviorally different from normal persons because they have *less* behavior, they are also behaviorally different because much of the behavior they exhibit occurs *inappropriately*—the child defecates or urinates on the floor or in his pants rather than in the toilet. If we want to have eliminative behavior occur appropriately, we must teach the child to defecate or urinate while sitting on the toilet with his pants down. The task for the trainer, then, is to teach him to eliminate only when sitting on the toilet with his pants down. When he will do this, we can say that elimination is now under *stimulus control* of the toilet and the pants in a pulled-down position with the child sitting on the toilet. Stimulus control is another important learning concept. The notion is that cues or stimuli in our environment control our behavior or make it occur. A dog urinates on a tree or a fireplug because the tree or the fireplug have become stimuli that control urination. Students bring pencil and paper to the classroom and sit at desks and take notes while the teacher lectures, because the teacher and the classroom have become stimuli that control sitting in desks and taking notes while the teacher talks. A boy kisses his girlfriend when he is sitting with her in his car at the drive-in movie because the girl, the car, and the drive-in movie have become stimuli that control kissing and other romantic things. The man driving his car puts his foot on the brake pedal and stops the car as he approaches a red traffic light, because the red traffic light has become a stimulus that controls putting on the brakes and stopping the car. When the light turns green, he takes his foot off the brake, places it on the accelerator and presses it down. The green traffic light causes him to put his foot down on the accelerator, because the foot is under stimulus control of the green traffic light. Similarly, a twenty mile per hour speed limit sign controls how fast we drive our car, just as a policeman in a patrol car does. A curve in the road to the right causes us to turn our steering wheel to the right as we approach it. When you drive down a city street or on the freeway, you steer your car between two white lines called lane lines. These lines control how you steer your car. If you are driving through a residential section and a child runs out in front of your car chasing a ball, you put on your brakes and stop to avoid hitting him. The child running in front of your car causes you to brake your car. You are driving down the road and notice your gasoline gauge registers empty. You happen to use Sunoco gasoline, so when you see a Sunoco sign, you slow down, pull into the gas station and ask for Sunoco gas. The gas gauge registering empty, plus the fact that you use Sunoco gasoline, plus the fact you see a Sunoco sign, all control your stopping at the station and asking for Sunoco gasoline. These are all examples of stimulus control.

All of the previous examples illustrate what happens when behavior is under *appropriate* stimulus control. However, what happens when behavior is under *inappropriate* stimulus control? We usually find the person under inappropriate stimulus control is violating some form of social taboo, either minor or major. The next two examples provide an illustration of what happens when behavior comes under inappropriate stimulus control. A young man is attempting to seduce a young woman in an inappropriate manner. He is using physical force to seduce her (rape). It is not the fact that he wants to engage in a sexual act with her that is inappropriate. Sexual interaction between men and women is very fashionable. It is the fact that he is using physical force to seduce her. Physical force in and of itself is not necessarily inappropriate. It is the circumstances under which it is occurring that makes it inappropriate. It is appropriate for a man to use physical force if he is a football player in a football game, if he is in a bar room brawl, if he is a policeman trying to arrest someone who will not submit peacefully to arrest, or if he is a soldier in combat defending himself from the enemy. But, it is not appropriate for a man to use physical force to seduce a woman in the typical American community. The man is doing the wrong thing in the wrong place and at the wrong time. He is under inappropriate stimulus control.

In order to bring this man under appropriate stimulus control, we must introduce some measure that will suppress or stop physical force and also teach him an appropriate way to seduce women. He needs to be taught to use sweet words consummated by mutual consent, i.e., he should ask her and obtain her permission. This is the appropriate way to seduce women.

In the second example, a man is attempting to obtain money from a bank using an inappropriate withdrawal procedure. He is attempting to withdraw money using a pistol. Again, it is not the pistol as such that is inappropriate. It is the context in which it is being used. It is acceptable for a bank guard to be in the bank with a pistol, or a guard from the Brink's Company to be in the bank with a pistol, or a policeman on duty to be in the bank carrying a pistol. But, it is not appropriate for an ordinary citizen to be in the bank wielding a pistol at a teller while requesting money. Also, it is all right for such a person to be out on a target range with a pistol or in the woods hunting game with a pistol. If this man is to be kept out of prison, he must be taught another way to make withdrawals from a bank while refraining from using a gun to make withdrawals. He must be taught to make withdrawals using a check—a check made out to him or from his own bank account with enough money in it to cover the amount written on the check. Many of the problem "psychotic" or "retarded" behaviors exhibited by children are caused by inappropriate stimulus control problems.

Stimulus control develops when a person performs some act in the presence of certain cues and receives reinforcement. If we want to teach our dog Spot to sit up to the cue, "Sit, Spot," we say, "Sit, Spot," get him somehow to sit and then reinforce him with a piece of meat and praise, e.g., "Good dog." After doing this a few times, Spot will sit up reliably to this verbal cue, and we have sitting up under stimulus control of the verbal cue, "Sit, Spot." Thus, if we want behavior to occur appropriately, we get it to occur under the appropriate circumstances, reinforce it, and cues in that situation will develop stimulus control over the behavior through a conditioning process. If we want to teach a child to eat his meal with a spoon rather than with his fingers, then we allow him to eat his meal only with a spoon. The spoon itself will then acquire stimulus control over eating his meal. The reinforcement that causes the spoon to acquire stimulus control properties is food.

SUMMARY

The two problems for the trainer who wants to make the retarded or autistic child act more like a normal person are (1) to teach him *more* behavior, and (2) to have the behavior occur under the *appropriate circumstances*. In order to teach *more* behavior, a *shaping-reinforcement* training technique is used. In order to see that behavior will occur *appro-*

priately, a *stimulus control-reinforcement* training procedure is used. Not only do we want to teach a child to take his pants off, we also want to teach him when and where to take his pants off—not in the classroom, not in the lunchroom, nor out on the playground. Rather, he should be taught to take his pants off at toileting time, bathtime and at bedtime.

Circle a T or an F in Front of Each Statement*

T F (1) The basic notion about stimulus control is that *cues* or *stimuli* in our environment control our behavior or make it occur.

T F (2) Stimulus control develops when a person performs some act in the presence of certain cues and receives reinforcement.

T F (3) A *stimulus control-reinforcement* procedure is used to teach children more or *new* behavior.

T F (4) A *stimulus control-reinforcement* procedure is used to get behavior to occur *appropriately*.

*Answers are on page 37.

Fill in the Missing Words*

(1) The operant conditioning method is primarily concerned with developing _____ behavior in children.

(2) Operant behavior is behavior that _____ on the environment to provide a person with reinforcement.

(3) Reinforcement is something like a reward that a child _____.

(4) Learning occurs because the child gets some kind of _____.

(5) Learning will *not* occur if the child being trained does *not* get _____ _____.

(6) The crucial factor that makes reinforcement effective for training is that the child is _____ to do something to get the reinforcement.

(7) A _____ is the requirement or thing a child has to carry out to get a reinforcement.

(8) _____ is a technique used to mold simple behavior into complex behavior.

(9) The _____ _____ procedure is used to teach a child a single piece or unit of behavior, like putting on a shirt or a pair of pants.

(10) A _____ procedure is used to teach a child a complex behavioral sequence, like dressing.

(11) A _____ _____ procedure is used to teach a child more or new behavior.

(12) The basic notion about _____ _____ is that cues or stimuli in our environment control our behavior or make it occur.

(13) A _____   _____   _____
       procedure is used to get behavior to occur appropriately.

Answers are on pages 37–38.

*Answer These Questions**

(1) What is operant behavior?
(2) What is a reinforcement?
(3) What is a reinforcement contingency?
(4) What is a shaping?
(5) When do you use a shaping-reinforcement procedure?
(6) What is stimulus control?
(7) When do you use a stimulus control-reinforcement procedure?

Answers are on page 38.

Answers to T-F, Fill-in, and Essay Questions

T-F on pages 22–23
- (1) T
- (2) F
- (3) T

T-F on page 25
- (1) T
- (2) T
- (3) F
- (4) T
- (5) T
- (6) T
- (7) T

T-F on pages 30–32
- (1) F
- (2) T
- (3) T
- (4) F
- (5) T
- (6) F
- (7) T
- (8) T
- (9) F

T-F on page 35
- (1) T
- (2) T
- (3) F
- (4) T

Fill-in on pages 35–36
- (1) voluntary
- (2) operates
- (3) likes
- (4) reinforcement

   (5)   reinforcement
   (6)   required
   (7)   contingency
   (8)   shaping
   (9)   successive approximation
 (10)   chaining
 (11)   shaping-reinforcement
 (12)   stimulus control
 (13)   stimulus control-reinforcement

Essay Questions on page 36

   (1)   Operant behavior is behavior that operates on the environment to provide the child with reinforcement.
   (2)   Reinforcement is something a child likes and will work to get.
   (3)   A reinforcement contingency is the requirement or thing a child has to carry out to get the reinforcement.
   (4)   Shaping is molding simple behavior into complex behavior.
   (5)   A shaping-reinforcement procedure is used to teach a child more or new behavior.
   (6)   Stimulus control refers to the fact that cues or stimuli in our environment control our behavior or make it occur.
   (7)   A stimulus control-reinforcement procedure is used to get behavior to occur appropriately.

CHAPTER 4

Shaping Behavior: I

As indicated in the previous chapter, the shaping technique makes it possible to teach complex behavior to autistic and retarded children. When the shaping technique is used in conjunction with a reinforcement procedure, one has a very effective method for teaching *new* behavior. The shaping technique is based upon two operant conditioning principles: *successive approximation* and *chaining*. Let us review successive approximation first.

SUCCESSIVE APPROXIMATION

The successive approximation technique is used to teach a *single* behavioral component, such as putting on a short-sleeved pullover shirt. As the illustrations in Fig. 4.1 indicate, putting on a short-sleeved pullover shirt can be taught using approximately five steps. Listed with the last step first, backward training order, you begin with the shirt completely on the child:

1. Have the child pull the hem of the shirt from about the rib cage down to the normal waist position (Fig. 4.1-1), and reinforce him with a "Good boy," said with a big smile and lots of enthusiasm, plus Koolade and candy or a snack and a pat on the back or a hug.
2. Have the child put his right arm into the right sleeve of the shirt while holding and pulling down on the shirt material just below the right sleeve (to facilitate getting the right arm into the right sleeve,

Fig. 4.1-2), pull the hem of the shirt down to the normal waist position, and reinforce him.

3. Have the child put his left arm into the left sleeve of the shirt while holding and pulling down on the shirt material just below the left sleeve (to facilitate getting the left arm into the left sleeve, Fig. 4.1-3), put his right arm into the right sleeve, pull the hem of the shirt down to the normal waist position, and reinforce him.

4. Have the child pull the shirt down over his head (Fig. 4.1-4), put his left arm into the left sleeve, put his right arm into the right sleeve, pull the hem of the shirt down to the normal waist position, and reinforce him.

5. The trainer hands the child the shirt so that he will grasp it by the hem with the front of the shirt facing his body (Fig. 4.1-5); the child pulls it down over his head, puts his left arm into the left sleeve, puts his right arm into the right sleeve, pulls the hem of the shirt down to the normal waist position, and is reinforced.

Training progresses at the child's own pace. You do not move to a new step until the child has mastered the previous step. Notice that the child always receives his main reinforcement when he completes the last step in the training sequence. Since he is being taught in a backward fashion, this is training step one (Fig. 4.1-1). If the child has difficulty learning the task, it is helpful to add more steps at the points where he has difficulty. *Prompts* also facilitate the learning process, i.e., the trainer helps the child to undress and later *fades* out or gradually eliminates the prompts. Prompting and fading will be considered in depth in Chapter 9, the chapter on stimulus control.

Verbal reinforcement is often used to keep the child moving when it looks like he may balk or stop in the middle of a training sequence, such as putting on a shirt. The trainer could say, "Okay, David, come on now, let's get that shirt on; that's a good boy, put it on now; hurry up David, let's go now; that's a good boy." This is an example of a verbal prompt.

A second example of the successive approximation procedure is teaching a child to put on his pants. This single behavioral unit can be taught in approximately eight steps. Beginning with the last step first, these are:

1. With his pants pulled up to his waist, the child grasps the waistband of his pants and is reinforced.

2. The child pulls his pants from a position halfway between the waist and the groin, up to the waist and is reinforced.

3. The child pulls his pants from the groin, to his waist and is reinforced.

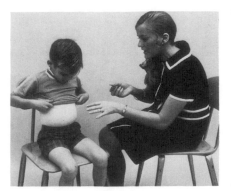

Fig. 4.1-1 The child pulls the hem of the shirt from his rib cage.

Fig. 4.1-2 The child puts his right arm into the right sleeve of the shirt.

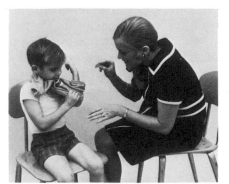

Fig. 4.1-3 The child puts his left arm into the left sleeve of the shirt.

Fig. 4.1-4 The child pulls the shirt down over his head.

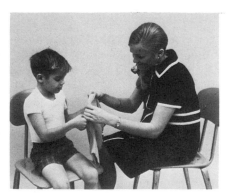

Fig. 4.1-5 The trainer hands the shirt to the child.

4. The child pulls his pants from his mid-thighs up to his waist and is reinforced.
5. The child pulls his pants from his knees up to his waist and is reinforced.
6. The child pulls his pants from his calves up to his waist and is reinforced.
7. With only one foot in his pants, the child puts in the other foot, pulls his pants up to the waist, and is reinforced.
8. The trainer hands the pants to the child in the waistband-up position with the back of the pants facing the child, the child puts in one foot, then the other foot, pulls them up to the waist, and is reinforced.

Some children can learn to put on this kind of pants in fewer than eight steps while others may require more. Additional steps are added at points of difficulty. As these two examples indicate, successive approximation consists of reinforcing closer and closer approximations to the desired behavior in a step-by-step fashion. As in the pants example, the child is required to do very little at first — only to grasp the waistbands of the pants. But gradually more and more is required of him until he can put on his pants completely when they are handed to him by the trainer. Notice the successive approximation procedure progresses in a *backward* fashion. It *begins at the training step immediately followed by reinforcement.* Although this backward approach to training may appear odd initially, the reader will find it is a very effective procedure.

A third example of successive approximation is teaching a child to put on a button-up shirt. Since buttoning itself is taught as a separate skill, training is limited to putting on the shirt and excludes buttoning *per se* (Fig. 4.2, page 45). Using a last step first, backward approach to training, the child would be taught to put on a button-up shirt in the following order:

1. He would pull the lapels of his shirt together (Fig. 4.2-1), and be reinforced with a "Good boy," said with a big smile and a lot of enthusiasm, followed by Koolade or candy, and a pat on the back or a hug (Fig. 4.2-2).
2. He would finish putting his left arm through the second sleeve of the shirt (Fig. 4.2-3), pull the lapels together, and be reinforced.
3. He would begin putting his left arm into the second sleeve of his shirt (Fig. 4.2-4), push his left hand all the way through the second sleeve, pull the lapels together, and be reinforced.
4. He would locate the opening to the second sleeve with his left hand (Fig. 4.2-5), put his left hand into the second sleeve, push it all the

way through the second sleeve, pull the lapels together, and be reinforced.

5. The child would hold the collar of his shirt with his right hand (this makes it easier for the left hand to locate the opening to the second sleeve) while his left hand searched for the opening to the second sleeve (Fig. 4.2-6); he would locate the opening to the second sleeve with his left hand, put his left hand into the second sleeve, push it all the way through the second sleeve, pull the lapels together, and be reinforced.

6. The child would finish pulling the first sleeve onto his right shoulder using his left hand (Fig. 4.2-7); he would hold the collar of his shirt with his right hand while his left hand searched for the opening to the second sleeve; he would locate the opening to the second sleeve with his left hand, put his left hand into the second sleeve, push it all the way through the second sleeve, pull the lapels together, and be reinforced.

7. The child would pull the first sleeve from his right elbow up onto his right shoulder (Fig. 4.2-8); he would hold the collar of his shirt with his right hand while his left hand searched for the opening to the second sleeve; he would locate the opening to the second sleeve with his left hand, put his left hand into the second sleeve, push it all the way through the second sleeve, pull the lapels together and be reinforced.

8. The child would pull the first sleeve of the shirt from his right wrist up onto his right shoulder (Fig. 4.2-9); he would hold the collar of his shirt with his right hand while his left hand searched for the opening to the second sleeve; he would locate the opening to the second sleeve with his left hand, put his left hand into the second sleeve, push it all the way through the second sleeve, pull the lapels together, and be reinforced.

9. The child would take the shirt from the trainer directing the right hand into the right sleeve while the left hand grasped the right sleeve (Fig. 4.2-10); he would pull the right sleeve of the shirt up onto his shoulder with his left hand; he would hold the collar of his shirt with his right hand while his left hand searched for the opening to the second sleeve; he would locate the opening to the second sleeve with his left hand, put his left hand into the second sleeve, push it all the way through the second sleeve, pull the lapels together, and be reinforced.

The size and number of steps used in the successive approximation procedure will depend upon how well the child is learning the behavioral step being taught. If he is learning rapidly, relatively few steps need to be employed. If he is learning with difficulty, the problem should be simplified by adding additional steps at the difficult steps of training, thus making each step smaller or requiring less of him at each step. For additional information about shaping behavior, *see* Ferster and Perrott (1968), Reese (1966), and Watson (1970).

Circle a T or an F in Front of Each Statement*

T   F   (1) The shaping technique is based upon two other operant conditioning principles: *shaping* and *successive approximation.*

T   F   (2) A successive approximation procedure is used to teach a *single behavioral component.*

T   F   (3) A successive approximation procedure would be used to teach a child to put on a shirt.

T   F   (4) Behavior is shaped in a backward fashion when a successive approximation training procedure is used.

T   F   (5) When behavior is shaped using a successive approximation procedure, the *last step* in the behavioral component is shaped *first.*

T   F   (6) If a child is taught to put on a short-sleeved pullover shirt using a *successive approximation procedure*, he will *first be taught to pull down the hem of the shirt to the normal waist position.*

T   F   (7) If a child is taught to take off his pants using a *successive approximation procedure*, he will *first be taught to remove them from only one ankle.* The trainer would pull the pants down until only one pants leg was hanging from one ankle. Then he would say, "Take off your pants," let the child remove the pants, and give him a reinforcement.

T   F   (8) When a child is trained using a *successive approximation procedure*, the *last step* in the behavioral component is the one followed immediately by reinforcement.

T   F   (9) If a child is taught to put on a short-sleeved pullover shirt using a *successive approximation procedure*, the *reinforcement* would be given *immediately* after he *pulled the hem of the shirt down to the normal waist position.*

T   F   (10) If a child is taught to take off his pants using a *successive approximation procedure*, the reinforcement would be given immediately after the *pants were removed from the last foot.*

**Answers are on page 50.*

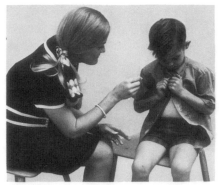

Fig. 4.2-1 The child pulls the lapels of the shirt together.

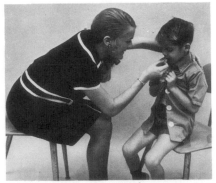

Fig. 4.2-2 The trainer reinforces the child.

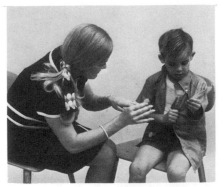

Fig. 4.2-3 The child finishes putting his left arm through the second sleeve of the shirt.

Fig. 4.2-4 The child begins putting his left arm into the second sleeve of the shirt.

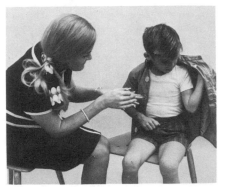

Fig. 4.2-5 The child locates the opening to the second sleeve of the shirt with his left hand.

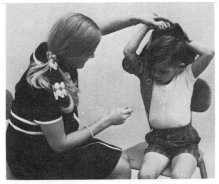

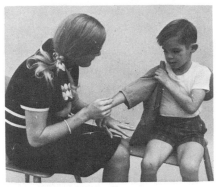

Fig. 4.2-6 The child holds the collar of the shirt with his right hand, while his left hand searches for the opening to the second sleeve.

Fig. 4.2-7 The child finishes pulling the right sleeve of the shirt onto his right shoulder.

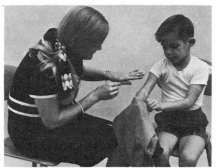

Fig. 4.2-8 The child pulls the right sleeve of the shirt from his right elbow up onto his right shoulder.

Fig. 4.2-9 The child pulls the right sleeve of the shirt from his right wrist up onto his right shoulder.

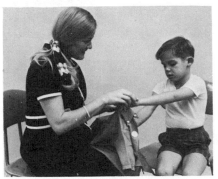

Fig. 4.2-10 The child takes the shirt from the trainer.

CHAINING

The chaining procedure is used to teach a complex behavioral unit, such as dressing in the morning. Dressing may consist of five single behavioral components:

1. putting on underpants;
2. putting on pants;
3. putting on a shirt;
4. putting on socks; and
5. putting on shoes.

Each of these five components are first conditioned singly using a successive approximation procedure. Then they are conditioned together, one at a time, using the same type of backward approach as with the successive approximation technique.

1. The trainer would begin by having the child put on his underpants, pants, shirt, and socks. Then he would say to the child, "Get dressed," have him put on his shoes, and reinforce him with a "Good boy," said with a big smile and enthusiasm, Koolade, candy or a snack, and a pat on the back or a hug.
2. Then he would have the child put on his underpants, pants, and shirt. He would say, "Get dressed," have him put on his socks for verbal reinforcement and his shoes for verbal reinforcement plus Koolade or candy and a pat on the back or a hug.
3. Next, the trainer would have the child put on his underpants and pants. He would say, "Get dressed," have him put on his shirt for verbal reinforcement, his socks for verbal reinforcement, and his shoes for verbal reinforcement, candy or Koolade, a pat on the back or a hug.
4. Then, the trainer would have the child put on his underpants. He would say, "Get dressed," have him put on his pants for verbal reinforcement, his shirt for verbal reinforcement, his socks for verbal reinforcement, and his shoes for verbal reinforcement, candy or Koolade, a pat on the back or a hug.
5. Finally, the child would be nude. The trainer would say, "Get dressed," have him put on his underpants for verbal reinforcement, his pants for verbal reinforcement, his shirt for verbal reinforcement, his socks for verbal reinforcement, and his shoes for verbal reinforcement, candy or Koolade, a pat on the back or a hug. After dressing behavior was well established, the trainer would drop out (or fade out) verbal reinforcement following putting on underpants,

pants, shirt, and socks and give reinforcement only after the child finished putting on his shoes.

The chaining procedure is important for two reasons: first, it allows the child to learn complex sequences of behavior; and second, it is very economical as far as reinforcement is concerned. You give only one main reinforcement after all behavior in the complex sequence has occurred. If each behavioral component in the preceding example can be thought of as a link, then the five links—(1) putting on underpants, (2) pants, (3) shirt, (4) socks, and (5) shoes—involved in this sequence make up the complex chain called dressing.

*Circle a T or F in Front of Each Statement**

T   F   (1) A *chaining* procedure is used to teach an *entire behavioral unit* by attaching a series of *behavioral components* together through conditioning.

T   F   (2) *Successive approximation* is used to teach an *entire behavioral unit* by attaching a series of *behavioral components* together through conditioning.

T   F   (3) A *successive approximation* procedure would be used to teach a child a complex behavioral unit, e.g., a dressing skill—putting on underpants, followed by putting on pants, followed by putting on a shirt, followed by putting on socks, followed by putting on shoes.

T   F   (4) A *chaining* procedure would be used to teach a child a *complex behavioral unit*, e.g., a dressing skill—putting on underpants, followed by putting on pants, followed by putting on a shirt, followed by putting on socks, followed by putting on shoes.

T   F   (5) A chaining technique is used to condition a series of *behavioral components* together using a backward conditioning approach.

Answers are on page 50.

*Fill in the Missing Words**

(1) The shaping technique is based upon two other operant conditioning principles: _____ and _____ _____.

(2) A _____ _____ procedure is used to teach a *single behavioral component.*

(3) A _____ procedure is used to teach a child a *complex behavioral unit.*

(4) A _____ procedure would be used to teach a child a complex behavioral unit, e.g., dressing—such as putting on underpants, followed by putting on pants, followed by putting on a shirt, followed by putting on socks, followed by putting on shoes.

(5) A _____ _____ procedure would be used to teach a child to put on a shirt.

(6) When behavior is shaped using a *successive approximation* procedure, the _____ step is taught *first*.

(7) If a child is taught to put on a short-sleeved pullover shirt using a *successive approximation* procedure, he will *first* be taught to _____

_____

This is the _____ step in the training sequence.

(8) If a child is taught to take off his pants using a *successive approximation* procedure, he will *first* be taught to _____

_____

This is the _____ step in the training sequence.

(9) When a child is trained using a successive approximation procedure, the _____ step in the *behavioral component* is the one followed immediately by reinforcement.

(10) If a child is taught to put on a short-sleeved pullover shirt using a *successive approximation* procedure, the reinforcement would be given immediately after he _____

_____

This is the _____ step in the training sequence.

(11) If a child is taught to take off his pants using a *successive approximation* procedure, the *reinforcement* would be given *immediately* after he

_____

This is the _____ step in the training sequence.

(12) When behavior is shaped using a chaining procedure, the _____ component is shaped *first*.

(13) When behavior is shaped using a *successive approximation* procedure, the child is reinforced when the _____ step is completed.

Answers are on page 50.

*Answer These Questions**

(1) What two operant conditioning principles make up the shaping technique?

(2) What are these two principles used for — specify the specific purpose *each* principle serves.

(3) Which component of a behavioral chain is taught first?

(4) When does the child get reinforced when a successive approximation training procedure is being used?

(5) Describe the successive approximation procedure in a step-by-step fashion.

Answers are on pages 50–51.

Answers to T-F, Fill-in, and Essay Questions

T-F on page 44
    (1) F
    (2) T
    (3) T
    (4) T
    (5) T
    (6) T
    (7) T
    (8) T
    (9) T
  (10) T

T-F on page 48
    (1) T
    (2) F
    (3) F
    (4) T
    (5) T

Fill-in on pages 48–49
    (1) chaining and successive approximation
    (2) successive approximation
    (3) chaining
    (4) chaining
    (5) successive approximation
    (6) last
    (7) pull the hem of the shirt down to the normal waist position; last
    (8) remove the pants from only one ankle or foot; last
    (9) last
  (10) pulled the hem of the shirt down to the normal waist position; last
  (11) removed the pants from only one ankle or foot; last
  (12) last
  (13) last

Essay Questions on page 49
    (1) Successive approximation and chaining.
    (2) The successive approximation procedure is used to teach a single

behavioral component or unit, e.g., to teach a child to put on a shirt or a pair of pants; while the chaining procedure is used to teach a complex behavioral sequence, e.g., dressing — putting on underpants, pants, shirt, socks, and shoes.

(3) The last.

(4) The child gets reinforced when the last step in training is completed.

(5) Using putting on a pullover shirt as an example, the child would be taught in the following manner:

  (a) The child would pull the hem of the shirt down to his waist from the rib cage position.

  (b) The child would put his right arm into the right sleeve of his shirt and pull the hem of the shirt down to his waist.

  (c) The child would put his left arm into the left sleeve of his shirt, his right arm into the right sleeve of his shirt, and pull the hem of the shirt down to his waist.

  (d) The child would pull the neck of the shirt down over his head, put his left arm into the left sleeve of his shirt, put his right arm into the right sleeve of his shirt, and pull the hem of the shirt down to his waist.

  (e) The trainer would hand the shirt to the child; the child would pull the neck of the shirt down over his head, put his left arm into the left sleeve of his shirt, his right arm into the right sleeve of his shirt, and pull the hem of the shirt down to his waist.

CHAPTER 5

Shaping Behavior: II

Now that we have discussed the two shaping principles, chaining and successive approximation, let us consider other aspects of shaping behavior. Before behavior can be shaped, *one must identify the behavior one wishes to shape.* Take toileting as an example. What is the *goal* of toilet training a child? It is to have him walk to the toilet (without being told to) when he is about to defecate or urinate, to pull down his pants and underclothing, and eliminate in the toilet. Once the goal of training has been identified, then it is possible to plan a training program. If the goal of training is not clearly determined, one cannot determine the steps that make up the final behavioral component. A second example of selecting the specific behavior one wishes to shape is taking off pants. One must ask the question, "When are pants off?" The answer is, of course, when they are off the child's body and legs and clear of his feet. Once this goal has been identified, the behavioral components that make up the behavior can be selected. *This final behavior, i.e., the shaping objective, is called the goal behavior or the target behavior.*

Circle a T or F in Front of Each Statement*

T F (1) It is *not* possible to plan a training program until the *goals* of training have been identified.

T F (2) *Goal behavior* is the final behavior to be shaped, or the *shaping objective* of training.

T F (3) One can easily select the training steps that make up the final behavioral component, even if the goal of training is *not* clearly determined.

T F (4) One cannot select the training steps that make up the final behavioral component until the *goals* of training are clearly determined.

T   F   (5) Once the goals of training are clearly determined, it is then possible to identify all training steps that are involved in shaping the final or goal behavior.

Answers are on page 61.

IDENTIFYING STEPS IN A BEHAVIORAL COMPONENT

The second step in planning a shaping procedure is to identify the steps that make up the behavioral component. Toileting, for example, can be broken down into twelve steps:

1. The child responds to his own bowel and bladder cues.
2. He inhibits or holds back elimination.
3. He walks from the room where he is located to the bathroom.
4. He opens the bathroom door and walks over to the toilet.
5. He pulls down his pants and underpants.
6. He sits on the toilet seat.
7. He defecates or urinates.
8. He cleans himself.
9. He gets up off the toilet.
10. He pulls up his underpants and pants.
11. He flushes the toilet.
12. He returns to the room where he was just prior to walking to the bathroom.

These are the steps that constitute the behavioral component called toileting. Success or failure of a training program will depend upon a correct, painstaking identification of all crucial steps that make up the behavioral component. If some essential steps are left out, the behavioral component may not develop properly. In general, *the more the behavior can be broken down into all its simple steps, the greater the chance will be that all children will learn the behavioral component.*

*Circle a T or F in Front of Each Statement**
T   F   (1) Success or failure of a training program will depend upon a correct, painstaking identification of all the crucial steps that make up the behavioral component.
T   F   (2) If some essential training steps are left out, the behavioral component may not develop properly.
T   F   (3) Leaving out one or two essential training steps will have little effect on the development or final outcome of a behavioral component.

Answers are on page 61.

OPERANT LEVEL

At this point, the child's existing behavioral level becomes quite important. The more deficient he is in behavior related to training him, the more steps will have to be shaped when teaching him any given skill. So, before training begins, it is necessary first to determine his existing behavioral level—does he pay attention when he is talked to, will he follow simple instructions, etc. This existing behavioral level is called the *operant level*. If he lacks these more basic behaviors, they first will have to be taught before other training can begin.

In summary, the first thing to do, before shaping complex behavior in a child, is to identify the goal behavior, determine the child's existing level of behavior or his operant level, and select the training steps that make up the behavioral component. One then uses the successive approximation principle to teach these component behaviors until the child can actually execute the goal behavior—as illustrated in the previous chapter on shaping.

Circle a T or F in Front of Each Statement*

T   F   (1) It is not particularly important to determine the child's *operant level* before identifying the important steps that will be used to shape the behavioral component of interest.

T   F   (2) It is very important to first determine the child's *operant level* before identifying the important steps that will be used to shape the behavioral component of interest.

T   F   (3) The *more deficient* he is in behavior involved in training him, the *more steps* will have to be *shaped* when teaching the child any given skill.

T   F   (4) Before a successive approximation procedure can be used to shape behavior, one must first identify the goal behavior, determine the child's existing operant level, and select the training steps that make up the behavioral component.

*Answers are on page 61.

STEPS IN SHAPING BEHAVIOR

With respect to the actual shaping or training process, there are several important steps to consider. These are summarized in Table 5.1. First, the trainer should *get to know the child* before she attempts to train him. Children usually do not work well with people with whom they are not acquainted. Children often will not follow instructions given by strangers even when they understand what they are supposed to do. Some are even

Table 5.1   Summary of Steps Involved in Shaping Behavior.

1. Get acquainted with the child.
2. Determine the child's reinforcement preferences. Use a reinforcement that is strong enough.
3. Shape attention.
4. Bring the child under simple verbal control, i.e., get him to follow simple instructions.
5. Determine the child's operant level.
6. Shape individual "pieces" of behavior, e.g., putting on a shirt, using a successive approximation procedure.
7. Shape complex sequences of behavior, e.g., dressing, using a chaining procedure.

afraid of strangers. One of the simplest ways to get acquainted with a child is to give him something he likes to eat and then have him perform simple tasks for reinforcement. Since all children do not like to eat the same things, the trainer should determine what will serve as a reinforcement for him, i.e., find out what he likes to eat. Most, but not all, like candy, many like cookies, potato chips, corn chips, cola, or Koolade. His reinforcement preferences are determined by offering him different foods until you find one he will eat. Now you have solved the most basic problem in training when you have found the kind of reinforcement that works with this particular child. Without such a reinforcement you cannot train him. The next step, and one which must be repeated during every step of training, is to get the child's *attention*. The trainer knows she has the child's attention when the child looks her in the eye or looks at the reinforcement. If he is not paying attention to the trainer, he will not learn or benefit from the training. So, the trainer always gets the child's attention first, i.e., his eye contact, and then tries to teach him something. This can be done by calling him by name, or by showing him the reinforcement or by clapping your hands together. Then, when he is looking at you or looking at the reinforcement, you can give your instructions and receive some kind of response if the child understands you. If he will not pay attention to the trainer he must be taught to pay attention before any other training can begin.

Assuming the trainer is acquainted with the child, has located a reinforcement that the child likes, and has found out how to get his attention, she is now ready to proceed with bringing him under verbal control, i.e., getting him to follow simple instructions. The first step is to stand about six feet from the child, hold the reinforcement out to him so he can see it, call his name to get his attention, and when he is either looking at the reinforcement or the trainer, say, "Come to me," and simultaneously gesture with your hands for him to walk over to you. Since the child has already tasted the candy, and knows he likes it, he will usually walk over to the trainer if he is not afraid of her. As soon as he reaches the trainer, she should say with a smile and enthusiasm, "Good boy, Billy!", hand him the reinforcement, and then pat him on the back while giving him words of praise. All three of these things, *candy*, *words of praise*, and a *pat on the back*, are reinforcements for most children. The extent to which words of praise, and a pat on the back will be effective reinforcements will depend on how enthusiastically the trainer gives them.

Some autistic and severely and profoundly retarded children do not understand spoken language very well, so other forms of communication are often necessary when training them. Two very effective ways are: (1) through gestures, and (2) through moving their body or limbs in the manner you want them to move to perform the desired act (*see* Fig. 5.1). Other simple tasks that can be used when getting acquainted with a child are to have him stand up and sit down. So, if the trainer wants such a child to sit in a chair, she shows him the reinforcement and calls him by name to get his attention and as soon as he is looking at her or at the reinforcement, she says, "Billy! Sit down, Billy!" and gestures with her hands in a downward direction and pats the seat of the chair. If he does not sit down, she gets his attention again by holding out the candy and calling his name, and as soon as he is looking at her or at the reinforcement, she says, "Billy! Sit down, Billy!" and gestures with her hands in a downward direction and pats the seat of the chair and then places a hand on his shoulder and gently pushes downward. As soon as he sits, she reinforces him with *enthusiastic praise* ("Good boy!"), *candy*, *and a pat on the back*. If she wants to get him to stand up after he is seated in the chair, she shows him the reinforcement and calls him by name to get his attention, and as soon as he is looking at her or at the reinforcement, she says, "Billy! Stand up, Billy!" and gestures with her hands in an upward motion and gently lifts his elbow. As soon as he stands up, she reinforces him with enthusiastic praise, candy, and a pat on the back.

In addition to getting acquainted with the child during this initial period when she is teaching him to follow simple instructions, the trainer is also showing him the "rules of the game" and the consequences of playing that game. If he follows her instructions, she will give him good things to eat and lots of attention and he will have fun.

After the trainer has found a reinforcement the child likes and will work for, has determined that she can get the child's attention, and has taught him to follow simple instructions for reinforcement, she is now ready

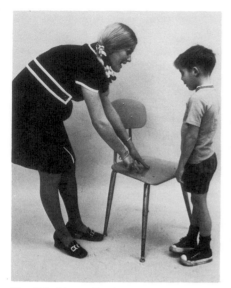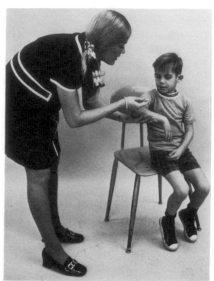

Fig. 5.1 Two effective ways to communicate with children are through gestures and through moving the body or limbs.

to begin teaching the child such skills as dressing, undressing, and toileting using the shaping method which utilizes the successive approximation and chaining techniques.

Two points should be considered further in this section. One is using a reinforcement that is powerful enough or strong enough to motivate the child to carry out training or to do the work required of him. When you are training a child, you are requiring him to expend energy or work, and the extent to which he will work is directly related to the value of the reinforcement for him. If the reinforcement is not powerful enough or strong enough, the child may not work for it, even though he will eat it if it is food, or play with it if it is a toy. A good illustration of this point is a one dollar bill. A dollar is a reinforcement for all of us who are called normal and has value for each of us. Yet, there are very few of us who will work all week for one dollar. Similarly, children have to have reinforcements that are powerful enough to get them to do the amount of work requested of them. Some children require more reinforcement to do the same amount of work than other children. In general, the more negativistic or apathetic the child, the more powerful the reinforcement must be to get him to put out a given amount of work.

The second point concerns *verbal communication* or using speech to direct and control the child. As already pointed out, some psychotic and retarded children do not understand verbal communication or speech very well. For this reason, it is suggested that if several people are working with such a child, a simple common language should be used. *Everyone* should use the *same* commands, in the same tone of voice with the same vocal inflections. This procedure helps ensure that the child will understand what is being said to him. It is also a good idea to keep the commands simple. An illustration of simple commands can be found in Table 5.2. Pairing gestures with verbal commands also helps the child to understand. Once the verbal commands acquire clearer meaning for the child, gestures can be eliminated.

Table 5.2 Simple Commands Used to Communicate Verbally with Children with Communication Disorders.

1. Come to me.
2. Stand up.
3. Sit down.
4. Take off your shirt (pants, etc.).
5. Put on your dress (pants, etc.).
6. Sit over there (said with a gesture).
7. Use your spoon.
8. Hold your fork (shirt, etc.).
9. Go to the potty.

SUMMARY

After the trainer has identified the goal behavior (the behavior he wishes to shape), determined the behavior components that constitute the complex goal behavior, and found out what the child's level of behavior is, she is now ready to begin training. The first step in training is to get acquainted with the child. The first thing to do when getting acquainted is to determine what reinforcements the child likes—candy, cookies, cola, Koolade, toys, or a hug. She then determines whether she can get the child's attention, and when she does, attempts to get him to follow simple instructions for reinforcement. When giving him instructions the trainer communicates in three ways: with words, gestures, and by moving the child's body or limbs. When he correctly complies with instructions, the child receives three kinds of reinforcement: candy or a cookie, Koolade or a toy, enthusiastic praise, and a pat on the back or a hug. After he will follow instructions for reinforcement reliably, he is now ready to be taught such skills as dressing, undressing, and toileting, using a shaping procedure (successive approximation and chaining).

Circle a T or F in Front of Each Statement*

T   F   (1) The trainer should get to know the child before she attempts to train him, since children often will not follow instructions from strangers even when they understand what they are supposed to do.

T   F   (2) It is not particularly important for the trainer to get acquainted with the child before she attempts to train him.

T   F   (3) Before reinforcement is used to train a child, the trainer should first determine his reinforcement preferences.

T   F   (4) It is important to always get the child's attention before trying to communicate with him.

T   F   (5) It is not necessary to get the child's attention before trying to train him.

T   F   (6) If the child is not paying attention to the trainer, he will not learn or benefit from training.

T   F   (7) Three ways to communicate with a child or get him to understand what you want him to do are through *talking*, *gestures*, and *movement of the child's limbs*.

T   F   (8) Three kinds of reinforcements used when training a child are: (a) candy or a toy, (b) praise, and (c) a pat on the back or a hug.

T   F   (9) Three ways to communicate with a child or get him to understand what you want him to do are: (a) candy or a toy, (b) praise, and (c) a pat on the back or a hug.

T   F   (10) Before attempting to teach a child a skill, such as putting on a shirt, the trainer should first get acquainted with the child, find out what reinforcement he likes, and get the child's attention each time before giving him instructions.

T   F   (11) It is important when training a child, to use a reinforcement that is strong enough to get him to do the work required of him.

*Answers are on page 61.

Fill in the Missing Words*

(1) _____   _____ is the final behavior or shaping objective of training.

(2) Once the goal of training is clearly determined, it is then possible to identify all training steps that are involved in shaping the _____ _____.

(3) Success or failure of a training program will depend upon a correct, painstaking identification of all the crucial steps that make up the _____ _____ _____.

(4) It is very important to first determine the child's _____

_____ before identifying the important steps that will be used to shape the behavioral component of interest.

(5) The *more deficient* he is in behavior involved in training him, the more _____ will have to be shaped when teaching the child any given skill.

(6) It is important to _____ _____ with the child before attempting to train him, since children do *not* work well for strangers.

(7) Before reinforcement is used to train a child, the trainer should first determine his _____ _____.

(8) It is important to always get the child's _____ before trying to communicate with him.

(9) If the child is not paying _____ to the trainer, he will not benefit from training.

(10) Three ways to communicate with a child or get him to understand what you want him to do are through _____, _____ _____, and _____ _____ _____ _____.

(11) The two most effective ways to communicate with a severely or profoundly retarded person are through _____ and _____ _____ _____ _____ _____.

(12) Three kinds of reinforcements used when training a child are: (a) _____ _____, (b) _____, and (c) _____ _____ _____ _____.

Answers are on pages 61–62.

*Answer These Questions**

(1) What is goal behavior?

(2) Why is it important to select all of the crucial steps that make up a behavioral component?

(3) What is the importance of the child's level of ability, when one begins shaping his behavior?

(4) Why is it important to get to know the child first before attempting to train him?

(5) Why should a child pay attention during training?

(6) What are the three main kinds of reinforcement one should use when training a child?

(7) What are the three ways a trainer can communicate with a child? Which two probably work best?

Answers are on page 62.

Answers to T-F, Fill-in, and Essay Questions

T-F on pages 52–53
- (1) T
- (2) T
- (3) F
- (4) T
- (5) T

T-F on page 53
- (1) T
- (2) T
- (3) F

T-F on page 54
- (1) F
- (2) T
- (3) T
- (4) T

T-F on page 59
- (1) T
- (2) F
- (3) T
- (4) T
- (5) F
- (6) T
- (7) T
- (8) T
- (9) F
- (10) T
- (11) T

Fill-in on pages 59–60
- (1) goal behavior
- (2) goal behavior
- (3) goal behavior
- (4) operant level

(5)   steps or behaviors
(6)   get acquainted
(7)   reinforcement preferences
(8)   attention
(9)   attention
(10)   words, gestures, and moving the child's limbs
(11)   gestures and moving the child's limbs
(12)   candy (or Koolade or a snack or toy), praise, and a pat on the back (or a hug)

Essay Questions on page 60.
(1)   Goal behavior is the final shaping objective or goal of training.
(2)   If any crucial steps are left out during training, the final behavior shaped may appear awkward or abnormal.
(3)   The greater the child's level of ability, the fewer the number of behaviors or behavioral steps he will have to be taught.
(4)   Children do not work well with strangers.
(5)   Children do not learn when they are not paying attention.
(6)   The three kinds of reinforcement used when training a child are: (a) candy or a snack or Koolade or a toy, (b) praise, and (c) a pat on the back or a hug.
(7)   The three ways to communicate with a child are through words or verbally, through gestures, and through movement of the child's body or limbs. Communicating through gestures and movement of the child's body or limbs probably works best.

CHAPTER 6

Reinforcement

Conditioning or shaping new behavior and bringing all behavior under appropriate stimulus control is accomplished through a reinforcement process. The success or failure of a training program will depend upon the effectiveness or power of the reinforcements used. So, it is very important to select reinforcements for each child that are powerful enough to make him respond to instructions to do such things as put on his shirt, take off his shirt, or use the toilet. The more powerful the reinforcement or the better the child likes it, the more work he is willing to do to get it, and the greater the likelihood the training program will be successful. Therefore, the first question one must ask when selecting a reinforcement for a child is whether it is powerful enough to get him to go through the training procedure and follow instructions.

As previously pointed out, a reinforcement is something a child likes such as candy, food, a toy or even an activity like riding on a merry-go-round or being held in an attendant's or a parent's lap. Since different children like different things, something that is a reinforcement for one child will not necessarily work with all children. Some children do not like candy and others do not particularly care to sit on an attendant's or a parent's lap while still others do. Something is called a reinforcement for a child *only* when he likes it and will work for it or put out some effort to get it. If he will *not* work to get it, then it is *not* considered to be a reinforcement for him.

Because different things serve as reinforcements for different children, we need some *rule of thumb* which can be used to decide what things are reinforcements for a particular child. The rule is that *if he will work or put out effort to get whatever is offered to him, then it must be a reinforcement. If he will not expend any effort to get it, then it is not a reinforcement.*

CONTINGENT REINFORCEMENT

Reinforcement is used when training children, because *reinforcement is necessary for learning to occur.* Reinforcement also energizes or motivates the negativistic, apathetic, or "do nothing" child to participate in a training program. It gets him off the chair or floor and starts him working. In addition, reinforcement provides the child with feedback. It lets him know he is performing satisfactorily in a training program. When he completes a step in training and gets reinforcement, he knows he is responding correctly.

However, it is not reinforcement alone that accounts for children learning new behavior in a training program. It is the *contingency* (or contract) that makes the important difference. Children learn desired behavior in a training program because they have to do something to get the reinforcement. *The thing they have to do to get the reinforcement is the contingency.* One illustration of a reinforcement contingency is the common example of a mildly retarded institutional resident who "panhandles" or "bums" money from institutional staff. A resident asks a nurse, "Loan me a quarter." The nurse replies, "If you want a quarter, make up all of the beds in this room, and I will give you one." The resident makes the beds, tells the nurse she is through, and then the nurse gives her a quarter. The contingency she had to satisfy to get the quarter was to make up the beds. The reinforcement, of course, was the quarter. The contingent reinforcement procedure is the most powerful and/or useful technique in the operant conditioning system. When used consistently and persistently, it will solve most of the problems encountered with children.

ACCELERATORS AND DECELERATORS

There are two kinds of consequences that can be used to change behavior: accelerators and decelerators. An accelerator is a reinforcement that gets behavior to occur and also speeds it up, such as candy or cookies or a hug or praise. Decelerators stop behavior from occurring or slow it down. These include different kinds of punishment, e.g., spanking a child. We use accelerators to get desirable behavior to occur, such as dressing, undressing, eating with a spoon, using the toilet, and talking; and we use decelerators to stop undesirable behavior, such as stealing food from a neighbor's plate, disrupting class, and attacking other children. Decelerators will be considered further in Chapter 8.

USING REINFORCEMENT EFFECTIVELY

There are four factors that will determine how effective reinforcement will be for controlling behavior. These are: (1) the *particular thing* being used as reinforcement, (2) the *time interval* between the occurrence of the behavior being shaped and giving the reinforcement to the child, (3) how long the child has been deprived of the reinforcement, and (4) the *size* of the reinforcement.

The Particular Thing Used as a Reinforcement

It is important that the child is given something he likes very much as a reinforcement. The particular thing offered to him will determine whether or not he will work to get it. Some children work best for food-type reinforcement; in fact, most prefer it. Most prefer sweet things to eat or drink. Others prefer starchy foods, such as crackers or potato chips. However, some children do not like to eat between meals and prefer a toy or a game or attention from a child or an adult they like. Meals are the most powerful reinforcements, and all children will work for their meals. So, the first consideration, when using reinforcement to train a child, is the particular thing to be used with that child.

The Time Interval Between the Occurrence of the Behavior
Being Shaped and Giving the Reinforcement to the Child

A second factor which determines how quickly and how well a child will learn a specific behavior is the speed with which he receives reinforcement after he makes the desired response. *Reinforcement always acts on the behavior that is occurring at the time it is given.* So, if a child is told to sit down, and he does, and then begins scratching his nose, and the reinforcement is given while he is scratching his nose, the effect of the reinforcement may be on the child scratching his nose. Then, the next time he is told to sit down, he may scratch his nose rather than sit down or he just may not sit down. Because the child will learn the behavior that is occurring at the time he gets his reinforcement, it is very important that he be given his reinforcement *immediately* after he makes the desired response. Ideally, the reward should be given within half a second, because a delay of one, two, three, or more seconds can have a detrimental effect on what the child learns and how quickly or how well he learns the thing the trainer is attempting to teach him. The longer the delay between sitting and getting the reinforcement, the longer it will take the child to learn to respond to the command, "Sit down."

This need for immediate reinforcement creates a problem for the trainer. It is impossible for most people to give a child a piece of candy, a bite of a snack, a drink of Koolade, or a toy in half a second or less. For this reason, a *bridging signal*, such as "Good boy," is needed. "Good boy" can be said at the moment the desired behavior is occurring and will serve as a bridge between the occurrence of the desired behavior and giving the main reinforcement — candy, a snack, Koolade, or a toy. Returning to the example of teaching a child to sit upon command, as soon as he sits, the trainer says, "Good boy," with a big smile and enthusiasm, hands him the candy as quickly as possible, and gives him a pat on the back or a hug.

Deprivation

The strength or power of a reinforcement will depend upon how long the child has been without it. A child who has just eaten a large meal will not crave food or even sweets as much as one who has not eaten for four hours. A child who has been deprived of food, candy, toys, or attention from others for a number of hours will crave these things more than one who has not been deprived of them. For this reason, we can make a reinforcement more effective or stronger by depriving the child before we begin training. Then he will work harder to get the reinforcement. When using particular snacks, toys, games, or specific kinds of attention as reinforcement, it is recommended that the child receive these things *only* at training time so he will work harder for them and learn faster.

Size of the Reinforcement

The opposite of deprivation is *satiation*. When a child has eaten his fill or has played with a toy all he wants to or has been given all the attention he wants, he is satiated, and at this point, he no longer craves it. For this reason, when training with reinforcements, such as candy, cookies, or potato chips, only small pieces should be used, since each time a child eats a piece he is a little more satiated and a little less deprived than he was before. The problem of satiation sets a limit on the number of reinforcements a child will work for during a single training period. If a child receives a whole candy bar for a single response, he may not work anymore for the rest of the training session. Thus, *reinforcement should not be too large.* On the other hand, if a reinforcement is *too small, the child may not work as hard* or put out as much effort to get it. As in the example of the dollar, if the child is not getting "union wages" he may "go on strike," that is, not work for the reinforcement. So, when we select our reinforcements for training, we try to keep them small enough in order that the child is not satiated too quickly, yet large enough to keep him working for it. This rule holds for all reinforcement: candy, snacks, attention, toys, and games of various kinds. In our own training programs, we usually limit attention to 5 seconds or less and games from 30 seconds to 1 minute. For further information about reinforcement, *see* Browning and Stover (1971), Ferster and Perrott (1968), Ferster and Skinner (1957), Gardner (1971), Honig (1966), and Premack (1959, 1965).

SUMMARY

The basic dimension of training children consists of accelerating appropriate or desirable behavior and decelerating inappropriate or undesirable behavior. Reinforcements that cause behavior to occur and increase it are called *accelerators*, while things that slow down behavior or stop it are called *decelerators*. Since particular things that serve as reinforcements vary from child to child, different things may have to be used as reinforcements for different children. A rule of thumb for selecting a reinforcement for a child is to determine if he will work to get it (accelerator) or will work to stop it (decelerator). Since *deprivation* makes a child work harder to get a particular reinforcement, he should be deprived of it prior to training. The *size* of the reinforcement is also important. If it is too large, the child will fill up on it quickly or become *satiated* and will stop working for it. If it is too small, he may not be willing to work for it at all. In order for reinforcement to be most effective, it should be given *immediately* after the behavior occurs since the child tends to learn what he is doing at the time he receives the reinforcement. Finally, reinforcement serves three functions in a training program: (1) it is responsible for learning occurring, (2) it motivates the child or gets him to work, and (3) it provides him with feedback or tells him that he is performing correctly in the training program.

*Circle a T or F in Front of Each Statement**

T   F   (1) Conditioning or shaping new behavior and bringing all behavior under appropriate stimulus control is accomplished through a reinforcement process.

T F (2) The success or failure of a training program can depend upon the effectiveness or power of the reinforcements used.

T F (3) The effectiveness or power of a reinforcement has little influence on the success or failure of a training procedure.

T F (4) The more powerful the reinforcement or the better the child likes it, the more he is willing to do to get it, and the greater the likelihood the training program will be successful.

T F (5) The first question one must ask when selecting a reinforcement for a child is whether it is powerful enough to get him to go through the training procedure and follow instructions.

T F (6) Something is called a reinforcement for a child if he likes it, *even* if he will *not* work to get it.

T F (7) Something is called a reinforcement for a child *only* when he likes it and will work or put out some effort to get it.

T F (8) There are two classes of reinforcement: *accelerators* and *decelerators*.

T F (9) There are two classes of reinforcement: *accelerators* and *negative activators*.

T F (10) An *accelerator*-type reinforcement *stops* behavior from occurring or *slows* it down.

T F (11) A *decelerator*-type reinforcement *stops* behavior from occurring or *slows* it down.

T F (12) An *accelerator*-type reinforcement *gets behavior to occur* and *speeds* it up.

T F (13) The effectiveness of a reinforcement will depend upon *how long* the child has been without it or *craves* it. This is called *deprivation*.

T F (14) As a child gets more and more of a reinforcement, he fills up on it. This is called *satiation*.

T F (15) As a child gets more and more of a reinforcement, he fills up on it. This is called *deprivation*.

T F (16) The problem of *satiation* sets a limit on the number of reinforcements a child will work for during a single training period. Children become *satiated* on large pieces of reinforcement faster than if they are given *small* pieces of reinforcement.

T F (17) If a reinforcement is *too small*, a child may not work to get it.

T F (18) The *size* of a reinforcement has no effect on *satiation*.

T F (19) The *size* of a reinforcement has no effect on whether or not the child *will work* to get it.

T F (20) The *time interval* between the occurrence of the behavior being shaped and giving the reinforcement has no influence on the *speed* with which he will learn the behavior.

T F (21) Since most trainers *cannot* hand a reinforcement to a child fast enough to promote rapid learning, a *bridging signal* is used.

T F (22) "Good boy" is an example of a bridging signal.

T   F   (23) A piece of candy is an example of a bridging signal.
T   F   (24) A bridging signal acts as a "bridge" between the completion of the behavior being shaped and the presentation of the main reinforcement.
T   F   (25) In order for a reinforcement to be most effective, it should be given *immediately* after the behavior occurs.

Answers are on page 71.

*Fill in the Missing Words**

(1) Conditioning or shaping new behavior and bringing all behavior under appropriate stimulus control is accomplished through a _____ process.

(2) The success or failure of a training program will depend upon the effectiveness or power of the _____ used.

(3) The more powerful the _____ or the better the child likes it, the more he is willing to do to get it, and the greater the likelihood the training program will be successful.

(4) The first question one must ask when selecting a reinforcement for a child is whether it is _____ enough to get him to go through the training procedure and follow instructions.

(5) Something is called a reinforcement for a child *only* when he _____ it and will _____ to get it.

(6) A _____ reinforcement *stops* behavior from occurring or *slows* it down.

(7) An _____ reinforcement gets behavior to occur and *speeds* it up.

(8) The longer a child has been without reinforcement the more he will _____ it. This is called _____.

(9) One way to make a reinforcement stronger or more powerful is to _____ a child of it.

(10) _____ occurs when a child is filled up on and no longer craves a reinforcement.

(11) When a child is _____ on a reinforcement, he will no longer work for it.

(12) If a reinforcement is too _____, a child may not work to get it.

(13) If a reinforcement is too _____, a child will fill up on it too quickly and no longer work for it.

(14) The _____ _____ between the occurrence of the behavior being shaped and giving the reinforcement will influence the *speed* with which he will learn the behavior.

(15) Since most trainers *cannot* hand a reinforcement to a child fast enough to promote rapid learning, a _____ _____ is used.

(16) _____ _____ is an example of a bridging signal.

(17) In order for a reinforcement to be most effective, it should be given _____ after the behavior occurs.

Answers are on pages 71–72.

Answer These Questions *

(1) Why is it important to use a reinforcement procedure when shaping new behavior and bringing all behavior under appropriate stimulus control?

(2) Why is it important to use a powerful enough reinforcement when training a child?

(3) What is a reinforcement?

(4) Will the same thing work as a reinforcement with all children?

(5) How can you tell whether something is a reinforcement for a child?

(6) What are the two classes or kinds of reinforcement?

(7) What is the importance of deprivation as far as reinforcement is concerned? What does it have to do with satiation?

(8) What is the importance of the size of a reinforcement for training?

(9) Why should a reinforcement be given immediately after the child does what the trainer wants him to do? What will happen if the trainer does *not* give it immediately?

(10) What is a bridging signal? Why use one?

Answers are on page 72.

Answers to T-F, Fill-in, and Essay Questions

T-F on pages 67–69

 (1) T
 (2) T
 (3) F
 (4) T
 (5) T
 (6) F
 (7) T
 (8) T
 (9) F
 (10) F
 (11) T
 (12) T
 (13) T
 (14) T
 (15) F
 (16) T
 (17) T
 (18) F
 (19) F
 (20) F
 (21) T
 (22) T
 (23) F
 (24) T
 (25) T

Fill-in on pages 69–70

 (1) reinforcement
 (2) reinforcement
 (3) reinforcement
 (4) powerful
 (5) likes; work
 (6) decelerator
 (7) accelerator
 (8) crave; deprivation

(9)   deprive
(10)   satiation
(11)   satiated
(12)   small
(13)   large
(14)   time interval
(15)   bridging signal
(16)   "Good boy"
(17)   immediately

Essay Questions on page 70

(1)   Reinforcement is necessary in order for learning to occur.

(2)   If the reinforcement is not powerful enough, the child will *not* work for it.

(3)   Reinforcement is something a child likes and will work to get.

(4)   All children do not like the same things as reinforcement, and therefore, all will not work for the same thing.

(5)   Something is a reinforcement for a child if he will work to get it or will work to stop it.

(6)   The two classes of reinforcements are accelerators and decelerators.

(7)   Deprivation makes the child work harder for the reinforcement. As the child gets each additional piece of reinforcement, he will fill up on it or become satiated, and crave it less. Once the child is satiated, he will no longer work for the reinforcement.

(8)   If the reinforcement is too large, the child will fill up on it quickly and stop working for it. If it is too small, he may not work for it at all.

(9)   Reinforcement acts on what the child is doing at the time he gets it. If it is not given immediately, he will learn more slowly or learn something other than the behavior the trainer wants to teach him.

(10)   A bridging signal, e.g., "Good boy," acts as a bridge between the occurrence of the child's desired behavior and giving him the main reinforcement. Bridging signals are used to increase how fast the child learns the task and how well he learns the task.

CHAPTER 7

Reinforcement: Accelerating Behavior

The purpose of this chapter is to further consider things that serve as reinforcements and accelerate behavior in children. We will look at reinforcement from several points of view. The first section will deal with reinforcement in terms of what the child does with it. He eats or drinks some reinforcements, while he plays with others. In the second section we will look at reinforcement from the standpoint of whether the child likes it the first time he is exposed to it, or has to be trained to like it. Then we will consider the reinforcement value of engaging in an activity or a task. Next, we will talk about reinforcement in terms of using things that are already in the child's daily life, as opposed to introducing novel outside things as reinforcement. Finally, we will consider how frequently reinforcement should be given in a training program.

THREE KINDS OF REINFORCEMENT

Edible Reinforcements

Things that children like which can be eaten or drunk are called *edible* reinforcements. Most children prefer something to eat or drink to games, attention from attendants or parents, or other activities. They like candy, cookies, jello, grapes, other kinds of fruit, baby food, custards, or regular meals. Types of candy they prefer are M & Ms, miniature malted milk balls, candy corn, and afterdinner mints. They like such snacks as Fritos, corn cheese, potato chips, pretzels, graham crackers, Lorna Doone cookies, ice cream, and sugar coated breakfast cereal. They also like to drink Coca Cola, orange juice, or Koolade. Since most children prefer these edible reinforcements, they will probably work harder for them than they will for toys, games, or attention. All children will work for their meals. There are, of course, children who do not crave sweets or snacks between meals and may prefer to play with a particular toy or play games. Different kinds of edible reinforcements are summarized in Table 7.1.

Manipulatable Reinforcements

Toys and games that do not involve other people make up a class of reinforcements called manipulatable reinforcements (*see* Table 7.1). Some children like to watch electromechanical toys move about, or they like to play with a ball or a doll. Still others may like to tear paper or cloth. Some may like to swing, climb a tree, take a shower, play in water, ride in a wheelchair, or ride a tricycle. As with edible reinforcements, if these things are to be used as reinforcements, the child should be deprived of them prior to training, and they should be allowed to play with them only for brief intervals during training, e.g., 30 seconds to 1 minute, if the trainer expects to administer such a reinforcement a number of times. Children also become satiated with toys and games or other kinds of manipulatable reinforcements just as they do with edible reinforcements.

Social Reinforcements

A third class of reinforcement is one that involves other people. Such reinforcements are called social reinforcements (*see* Table 7.1). Parents, teachers, or nurses can give children praise, hugs, a pat on the back, hold them in their laps, and play games with them. If an attendant swings a child around, this may be a social reinforcement for that particular child. If she pushes him in a wheelchair or pulls him in a wagon, this is a combination *social-manipulatable* reinforcement. Again, *deprivation* and *satiation* should be considered when using this kind of reinforcement.

Circle a T or F in Front of Each Statement*

T F (1) Most children prefer something to eat or drink to games or attention from an attendant or parent.

T F (2) Three classes of reinforcements are: (a) things to eat and drink, (b) toys and games, and (c) a pat on the back or a hug.

T F (3) All three classes of reinforcements listed in statement #2 are effected by *deprivation* and *satiation*.

T F (4) Only things that the child can eat and drink are effected by *deprivation* and *satiation*.

*Answers are on page 85.

Table 7.1   Summary of Accelerator-type Reinforcements.

Edible	Manipulatable	Social
Meals	Ride in wagon	Praise
baby food	Ride on tricycle	Kisses
Candy	Ride in Krazy Kar	Hugs
jelly beans	Ride in Toy Car	Sit in lap
mints	Ride in wheelchair	Be patted or stroked
M & Ms	Ride on "train" or bus	Hear a story
gum drops	Ball	Play a game with peers
candy corn	Simple game	Be swung around
malted milk balls	Small toy, car, or truck	Be chased
chocolate	Formboard puzzles	Smiles
Ice cream	Coloring	Applause
Milk shakes	Cutting and pasting	"Simon Says"
Cookies	TV-music box toy	Singing songs
Crackers	Trampoline	Dancing
cheese crackers	Jungle gym	
saltine crackers	Teeter totter	*Tokens*
graham crackers	Merry-go-round	Money
Dry, presweetened breakfast	Swing	Bib
cereals	Sliding board	Poker chips
Fruit	Swimming	Token sheets
raisins	Shower or bath	Ticket
apples	Music	
oranges	Television	
pears	Look at a book	
grapes	Look at a magazine	
Pretzels	Run an errand	
Fritos	Play in water	
Potato chips	Flushing toilet	
Cheese twists	Rhythm instruments	
Bugles	Going outside to play	
Whistles	Flashing light box	
Koolade	Hot Wheels	
Coca Cola	Blow gun	
Orange juice	Dart gun	
Milk	Ropes and Ladders (board game)	
Chocolate milk	Candy Land (board game)	
Water	Taking a walk	
Coffee	Setting the table	
Peanut butter cups	Electrical toys that move	
Peanut butter	and make sounds and	
Tea	have flashing lights	

UNCONDITIONED VERSUS CONDITIONED REINFORCEMENT

Another way to classify reinforcement is on the basis of whether it is unlearned or learned. Using psychological jargon, we say reinforcements are *unconditioned* or *conditioned*. An *unconditioned reinforcement* is *unlearned*. The child likes it the first time he is introduced to it. Candy, fruit, meat, milk, crackers, and cookies are examples of unconditioned reinforcement.

A *conditioned reinforcement* is something that originally had little or no value for a child, but as a result of being associated with other reinforcements, the child learns to like it, and it becomes a reinforcement in time. *Conditioned* means *learned*. Thus a *conditioned reinforcement* is a *learned reinforcement*. If a child is given poker chips, which initially may have little value for him, and he exchanges them for candy and things he likes, he will learn to like the poker chips for their purchase value. Because they can be used to purchase candy and other good things, they will soon acquire reinforcement value for the child and may become a very powerful reinforcement. Money serves the same function for normal people. It initially has very little value for very small children, but they learn to like it because they see their parents buy things with it, and they later use it to buy candy, pop, and other good things. Thus, money acquires value for people because of the things it will buy. Trading stamps and cigarette coupons are other examples of *conditioned reinforcement*.

Another example of conditioned reinforcement is a bib. Small retarded children at the Columbus State Institute are required to wear a bib when they eat their meals. Children are *not* allowed to enter the dining room until they are wearing their bibs. The bibs become the tickets that get them into the dining room. Because the bibs are always worn during mealtime (a very reinforcing time), and because the child must have it on to enter the dining room, the bib becomes a very powerful conditioned reinforcement, even though initially it may have no reinforcement value.

Sometimes a child may initially have to be reinforced to motivate him to play a certain game. Yet, with time, if he is getting enough reinforcement for playing the game, the game itself may become fun for the child because of the reinforcement it provides him. The game itself develops into a *conditioned reinforcement*. When this happens, the child may no longer have to be given reinforcement to play the game since the act of playing the game itself has become reinforcing and may also produce other reinforcements, e.g., social reinforcement.

The way a conditioned reinforcement is learned is by pairing it or associating it with an *unconditioned* reinforcement or another *condi-*

tioned reinforcement. The originally unreinforcing object or thing becomes conditioned to be a reinforcement as a result of the association between the "to be conditioned" reinforcement and the unconditioned reinforcement.

Conditioned reinforcement offers one important advantage over unconditioned reinforcement. It is less influenced by *satiation* effects *if* it is a *generalized* conditioned reinforcement. A *generalized conditioned reinforcement* is one that has been associated with several unconditioned reinforcements such as money, poker chip tokens, or praise. Money and poker chip tokens are influenced very little by specific satiation effects because they will purchase a large number of unconditioned reinforcements, and it is highly unlikely that the child will ever be satiated on all unconditioned reinforcements that the tokens or money will purchase—if a large number and variety of items are available for exchange to the child.

Conditioned reinforcements may lose their reinforcement value if they are *not* periodically paired or associated with unconditioned reinforcement. They gain their value or reinforcement strength as a result of being paired with unconditioned reinforcement, and may lose their strength through use unless they are occasionally "recharged" with unconditioned reinforcement, just as a battery must be periodically recharged by a generator.

In conclusion, since edible reinforcements are about the only unconditioned or unlearned reinforcements available, it is essential that other things are conditioned to be reinforcements for children. Because a large number of reinforcements are required to operate a 24-hour, seven day a week training program for children, conditioned reinforcement must be employed to keep the child involved in the program throughout the day, day after day. Conditioned reinforcements allow the trainer access to a virtually limitless supply of reinforcements.

*Circle a T or F in Front of Each Statement**

T   F   (1) A *conditioned reinforcement* is one which originally had little value for the child, but as a result of being paired or associated with other reinforcements, acquired reinforcement value.

T   F   (2) Poker chips that can be exchanged for candy and other goodies are an example of a *conditioned reinforcement*.

T   F   (3) A bib is another example of a *conditioned reinforcement*.

T   F   (4) A piece of candy is still another example of a *conditioned reinforcement*.

T   F   (5) Money is an example of a *conditioned reinforcement*.

T   F   (6) A meal is an example of a *conditioned reinforcement*.

T   F   (7) An *unconditioned reinforcement* is one that already has value for the child the first time he is introduced to it, and does not have to be learned.

T   F   (8) Candy is an example of an *unconditioned reinforcement*.

T   F   (9) A bib is an example of an *unconditioned reinforcement*.

T   F   (10) Milk is an example of an *unconditioned reinforcement*.

T   F   (11) A poker chip that can be exchanged for candy or other goodies is an example of an *unconditioned reinforcement*.

T   F   (12) A *conditioned reinforcement* is a reinforcement that the child learns to like because it is associated with other reinforcements, while an *unconditioned reinforcement* is one the child already likes when he is first exposed to it.

T   F   (13) A *conditioned reinforcement* is one the child already likes when he is first exposed to it, while an *unconditioned reinforcement* is a reinforcement that the child learns to like because it is associated with other reinforcements.

Answers are on page 85.

REINFORCEMENT VALUE OF A TASK

The kinds of reinforcements we have discussed so far are those which a child is given for doing something or completing a task. There is still another different kind of reinforcement. This is the *reinforcing value of the task itself*. Some activities are fun. It is sometimes possible to get a child to engage in an activity simply because he enjoys it. Many children will sing, dance, clap their hands in time to music, work puzzles, run errands, sort clothes, sweep floors, and make beds because they enjoy such kinds of activity. The activity may provide them with pleasure or a sense of satisfaction as well as with prestige among the other children on their ward, or in their school, and no other reinforcement may be needed to maintain such behavior.

In contrast to activities or tasks which are enjoyable to children, some can become monotonous or boring. Tasks initially can be reinforcing and enjoyable, but with time, they may become monotonous. Children may initially complete these tasks for reinforcement, but with time, refuse to engage in them, even for reinforcement. It may be that the child is initially under deprivation for this kind of activity, becomes gradually satiated with it, and then it actually becomes unpleasant to him.

Circle a T or F in Front of Each Statement*

T   F   (1) The act of performing a *task* can be *reinforcing* to a child, e.g., running errands.

T   F   (2) Some tasks may be very monotonous or boring to some children.

*Answers are on page 85.

ARTIFICIAL VERSUS NATURAL REINFORCEMENT

Most of the reinforcements we have considered so far are very useful for training purposes, i.e., for teaching children new behavior. Things like candy, cookies, Koolade, and toys that are used to teach children dressing skills, language skills, educational skills, and social skills are called *artificial* reinforcements. They are called artificial because they are not usually used in more normal, real-life situations. Most mothers do not give children candy or cookies for dressing or for doing their homework or completing their chores. Such reinforcements are not natural or indigenous to most home, school, or institutional situations. However, such reinforcements are extremely important for teaching children new behaviors such as dressing skills or toileting skills.

Once a child has learned new behavior, we need some reinforcement that will maintain the behavior, but it should be one that is natural to the situation, one that is usually found in that situation. Two common examples of natural reinforcement are mealtime and playtime or recreational activities. They already exist in the institution, home, and in most school situations. We have used a bib as a reinforcement for getting up in the morning, going to the bathroom, and getting dressed at Columbus State Institute. The child does not get his bib until he has completed these activities. Without his bib, he will not be allowed to go to breakfast. We also toilet trained a very negativistic autistic child using a bib as a reinforcement. He could not get his bib until he urinated in the toilet. Without his bib, he could have neither meals nor snacks. His frequency of wetting was reduced to almost zero after this contingency was introduced.

We made playtime contingent upon completion of tablework in our preschool at Columbus State Institute. In order to be allowed to go to the playroom and play with toys, each child was required to complete the project he was assigned, have it approved by the teacher, put all work materials back in their proper storage area, and *only* then was he allowed to walk through the door to the playroom. Once he was in the playroom, he could take a toy from a storage area, go over to a table, and play with it for the rest of the class period. At the end of the class period, the child put the toy back on the appropriate shelf in the storage area, and returned to the regular classroom. If he misused the toy or interfered with other children in the playroom, he was expelled from the playroom for the remainder of that play period. By making playtime contingent upon completion of tablework, children completed their tablework more promptly and the class went more smoothly.

Natural reinforcement has certain advantages over artificial reinforcement. First, it is more economical. It costs less money to use since it is already there. Second, parents and teachers are more likely to use it since it seems to be less novel or strange to the situation. Many mothers have been applying natural contingent reinforcement techniques for years anyway. Third, natural reinforcement insures the durability of the behavior, since it is indigenous to that situation and will always be there and requires only that it be made available on a contingent basis. In contrast, artificial reinforcement has to be brought into the situation and is easily forgotten. Finally, when natural reinforcement is used, the entire behavioral situation looks more "natural" and less strange to others. In conclusion, *artificial reinforcement is used to shape new behavior, while natural reinforcement is used to maintain it once it is acquired.*

Circle a T or F in Front of Each Statement*

T F (1) A *natural reinforcement* is one already present in the daily ward or home routine of the child.

T F (2) A *meal* is an example of *natural reinforcement.*

T F (3) A *poker chip* that can be exchanged for candy is an example of a *natural reinforcement.*

T F (4) A piece of candy is an example of a *natural reinforcement.*

T F (5) *Playtime* or *recreation* is an example of a *natural reinforcement.*

   *Answers are on page 85.

CONTINUOUS VERSUS INTERMITTENT REINFORCEMENT

Another way to classify reinforcement is on the basis of how often it is given to the child. There are two basic ways to give reinforcement: *every time* the child does what we want him to, and *less than every time* he performs a task. The first is called *continuous reinforcement* and the second is called *intermittent reinforcement.* When we are teaching a child a new task, we give him reinforcement every time he does what we tell him to. We say, "Good boy," with enthusiasm, give him candy or a cookie or a toy, and a pat on the back or a hug. After the child learns the task, we may continue to say "Good boy" every time the child completes the task, but we usually give him candy and a hug only every fifth or tenth time he completes the task or we may even omit the candy, cookie, or toy reinforcement completely. When we are chaining a series of behaviors together, we usually say "Good boy" to the child as he completes each component of the chain, but give him candy or a cookie or a hug or pat *only* after he completes the entire sequence. For example, if we are chaining a series of individual dressing skills together to make up a dressing sequence, we could say "Good boy" after he put on his underpants, say "Good boy" after he put on his pants, say "Good boy" after he put on his shirt, say "Good boy" after he put on his socks, and say "Good boy" after he put on his shoes, and give him a pat on the back, and his bib, which would then qualify him to go to breakfast. Once the child had learned the dressing sequence well, we would eliminate all "Good boys" except the one that followed putting on the child's shoes, the last component in the chaining sequence. Once a child has learned a task well, he does not need as much reinforcement to get him to carry it out. So we usually omit candy or cookies or a toy, and find that many children will work just for praise and a hug—although some will not. Intermittent reinforcement is more economical than continuous reinforcement.

Intermittent reinforcement has two additional advantages over continuous reinforcement. It produces greater resistance to extinction. The child will work for a longer period without reinforcement after being on intermittent reinforcement than after being on continuous reinforcement. Intermittent reinforcement can also be used to increase the *speed* with which the child responds, and also the *pattern* of responding. If a response is reinforced on a piecework basis, e.g., every fifth time he responds, the child will work faster. If the child is reinforced on a time basis, he will work faster or slower depending on how often he is reinforced, and this will determine the total response pattern.

*Circle a T or F in Front of Each Statement**

T   F   (1) There are two ways to give reinforcement to a child: *every time* he does what we want him to or *less than every time.*

T   F   (2) When we are teaching a child a *new task* or *skill*, we typically give him *reinforcement every time* he does what we tell him to.

T   F   (3) After a child has learned a *skill well*, we usually give him reinforcement *less than every single time* he completes the task.

Answers are on page 85.

TWO FUNCTIONS SERVED BY REINFORCEMENT

Reinforcement serves two functions in training. First, it gets the child to follow instructions or carry out a task, since through experience, he comes to expect reinforcement for completing the task. Reinforcement *motivates* him. Second, reinforcement lets him know he has completed the task correctly, since he does not get reinforced when he does it incorrectly. Reinforcement provides him with *feedback*. Once he has learned the task well, he is less dependent on the reinforcement to let him know he is right. That is one important reason why continuous reinforcement should be used while a child is learning a skill, but intermittent reinforcement is sufficient to maintain the skill once the child learns it well. Continuous reinforcement supplies the child with greater feedback than intermittent reinforcement. He does not need as much feedback after he has learned the task. For additional information about reinforcement, *see* Baer and Wolf (1970), Browning and Stover (1971), Ferster (1967), Ferster and Perrott (1968), Ferster and Skinner (1957), Gardner (1971), Honig (1966), Lent, LeBlanc, and Spradlin (1970), Reese (1966), Spradlin and Giradeau (1966), and Watson (1970).

SUMMARY

There are three main kinds of reinforcement. First, there are those which the child eats or drinks. These seem to be the most powerful. Then there are those he plays with by himself, such as toys and games that do not involve other people. Finally, there are those which involve people, such as praise, attention or physical contact from an attendant or parent or another child. All three of these reinforcements are subject to deprivation and satiation effects. In addition to these reinforcements that are given for completing a task, the task itself can serve as a reinforcement — if the child enjoys it. There are also reinforcements that originally have little or no value but acquire value as a result of learning. These are conditioned reinforcements. There are reinforcements that are unlearned, i.e., they are reinforcing to the child the first time he is exposed to them. These are unconditioned reinforcements. Once a child has learned a behavior, reinforcement already present in the daily routine can be used to maintain behavior. This is called natural reinforcement as opposed to artificial reinforcement. Reinforcement can be given to a child in two ways: every time he does what he is told to and less than every time. The first is called continuous reinforcement and the second intermittent reinforcement. Finally, reinforcement serves two functions in training: it motivates the child to carry out the task, and it lets him know he has completed the task correctly.

Circle a T or F in Front of the Statement*

T   F   (1) Reinforcement serves two functions in training: it gets the child to follow instructions or carry out a task, and it lets him know he completed the task correctly.

*Answer is on page 86.

Fill in the Missing Words*

(1) Three classes of reinforcement are: (a) _____, (b) _____, and (c) _____.

(2) All three classes of reinforcement listed in #1 are effected by _____ _____ and _____.

(3) A _____ reinforcement is one that originally had little value for the child, but as a result of being paired or associated with other reinforcements, acquired reinforcement value.

(4) An _____ reinforcement is one that already has value for the child the first time he is introduced to it and does *not* have to be learned.

(5) Poker chips that can be exchanged for candy and other goodies are an example of a _____ _____.

(6) A piece of candy is an example of an _____ _____ _____.

(7) Money is an example of a _____ _____.

(8) Coca Cola is an example of an _____ _____.

(9) The act of performing a task can be _____ to a child.

(10) A _____ reinforcement is one already present in the regular daily ward or home routine of the child.

(11) A meal is an example of a _____ reinforcement.

(12) Playtime or recreation time is an example of a _____ reinforcement.

(13) There are two ways to give reinforcement: _____ _____ a response occurs and _____ _____ every time it occurs.

(14) When we are teaching a child a *new task* or *skill*, we typically give him reinforcement _____ _____ he does what we tell him to.

(15) After a child has learned a *skill well*, we usually give him reinforcement _____ _____ _____ _____ he completes the task.

(16) Reinforcement serves two functions in training: (a) _____, and (b) _____.

*Answers are on page 86.

Answer These Questions*

(1) What are the three main kinds of reinforcement? Do *not* use the answer to questions #2 and #3.

(2) What is the difference between a conditioned and an unconditioned reinforcement?

(3) What is a natural reinforcement? How does it differ from other reinforcements usually used in training?

(4) What are the two ways to give reinforcement?

(5) What two functions does reinforcement serve during training?

Answers are on page 86.

Answers to T-F, Fill-in, and Essay Questions

T-F on page 74
    (1) T
    (2) T
    (3) T
    (4) F

T-F on pages 77–78
    (1) T
    (2) T
    (3) T
    (4) F
    (5) T
    (6) F
    (7) T
    (8) T
    (9) F
   (10) T
   (11) F
   (12) T
   (13) F

T-F on pages 78–79
    (1) T
    (2) T

T-F on page 80
    (1) T
    (2) T
    (3) F
    (4) F
    (5) T

T-F on page 81
    (1) T
    (2) T
    (3) T

T-F on page 83
> (1)   T

Fill-in on page 83
> (1)   edibles (or things to eat), manipulatables (or things children play with), and social (or things that involve people)
> (2)   deprivation; satiation
> (3)   conditioned
> (4)   unconditioned
> (5)   conditioned reinforcement
> (6)   unconditioned reinforcement
> (7)   conditioned reinforcement
> (8)   unconditioned reinforcement
> (9)   reinforcing
> (10) natural
> (11) natural
> (12) natural
> (13) every time; less than
> (14) every time
> (15) less than every time
> (16) motivation; feedback

Essay Questions on pages 83–84
> (1)   The three main kinds of reinforcement are edible (things to eat and drink), manipulatable (things children play with), and social (things that involve people).
> (2)   A conditioned reinforcement is a learned reinforcement, while an unconditioned reinforcement is unlearned, i.e., the child likes it the first time he is introduced to it.
> (3)   A natural reinforcement is one already present in the daily home or institutional life of the child. Reinforcements usually used to teach children new behavior are artificial to the situation, e.g., candy or cookies.
> (4)   Two ways to give reinforcement are every time the behavior occurs or less than every time it occurs.
> (5)   The two functions reinforcement serves during training are motivation and feedback.

CHAPTER 8

Decelerating Behavior

Accelerator reinforcement, such as candy, cookies, hugs, and praise, may be useful for teaching children new behavior, but accelerator reinforcement by itself is usually not effective for eliminating undesirable behavior. When we want to control certain behavior like breaking out windows, hitting another child, or hitting oneself in the head, there are three basic steps that can be taken. The first step is to reduce the child's eight basic psychobiological deprivation states (to be explained later). Any excessive stress conditions that are causing frustrations should be eliminated. Second, the child should be taught an appropriate way to express his anger when he is frustrated. Third, if the undesirable behavior still exists, one or more of five techniques specifically designed to eliminate undesirable behavior can be employed. These are: (1) extinction, (2) satiation, (3) avoidance of the situation that causes the undesirable behavior, (4) conditioning an incompatible response, and (5) use of "therapeutic" punishment.

REDUCING PSYCHOBIOLOGICAL DEPRIVATION STATES

All children have certain *psychobiological* needs or deprivation states which must be satisfied on a regular basis. These are: (1) the need for attention or recognition from parents, teachers, other important adults, and peers or playmates; (2) the need to satisfy their curiosity; (3) the need for physical activity; (4) the need to maintain comfortable temperature and humidity levels; (5) the need for bladder and bowel elimination; (6) the need for food and water; (7) the need to reduce or eliminate fatigue;

87

and (8) the need to satisfy the sexual drive as puberty approaches. Whenever any of these need states are unsatisfied and are at a high level, they drive the child into activity directed toward satisfying that particular deprivation state. Children labeled as "hyperactive" or "brain damaged" may be running around the ward or home and getting into everything because of a special need for physical activity or a special need to satisfy their curiosity. Children who engage in a variety of undesirable behaviors, e.g., smearing feces, pinching another child, mother or an attendant, crying and whining, or having temper tantrums, may be doing these things because they have a high deprivation state for attention.

By planning activities in the child's daily routine that will satisfy these psychobiological deprivation states, many behavioral problems exhibited by autistic and retarded children will be eliminated. So, the first step in eliminating undesirable behavior in a child is to plan a full day's activities to keep the child occupied (reduce his curiosity deprivation state and avoid boredom), satisfy his need for attention, reduce his need for physical activity, as well as the other psychobiological deprivation states. Children identified as hyperactive may need more attention, more opportunities to satisfy their curiosity, and more frequent activity periods each day, than other children.

CONTROLLING FRUSTRATION

All people become frustrated, and all people become angry. It is quite normal to be both frustrated and angry from time to time. Problems concerning frustration arise when a person becomes frustrated too frequently and expresses his anger caused by the frustration in an inappropriate manner. Three steps can be taken to reduce the problem of frustration in children. First, steps should be taken to increase the child's frustration or stress tolerance. Second, steps should also be taken to eliminate any unreasonable stress to the child, and third, the child should be taught an appropriate way to express his anger. The first step requires development of a program to gradually increase the child's ability to tolerate frustration. Next, steps should be taken to eliminate unreasonable frustration. An important source of frustration with children is boredom. They do not have enough interesting or stimulating activities to keep them occupied. Such a child needs a full day's activities to keep him from being bored. Another source of frustration may be due to a physical disorder. We found that a child with frequent temper tantrums had an impacted colon. He often cried and had tantrums when he sat down. By eliminating the physical problem, we reduced the frequency of temper tantrums. Fatigue can also cause frustration and inappropriate behavior. Excessive frustration can be caused by bullying from other children or requiring the child to carry out a task for which he is not equipped, e.g., an educational or work task that is too difficult for the child.

The third problem, expressing anger appropriately, should be attacked from two directions: physical expression of anger and verbal expression of anger. Many children exhibit inappropriate ways of expressing their anger physically. Some may attack themselves, e.g., beat themselves about the head or face with their fists and their knees, or beat their heads against the wall, floor, or furniture. Others attack other children when they are angry, destroy toys or furniture, break out windows, or kick holes in doors. They need to be taught an acceptable outlet for physically expressing their anger. We taught a headbanger at Columbus State Institute to hit someone else's hand when he was angry. Children who attack other children, destroy furniture, or break windows can be taught to hit a punching bag, tear paper or cloth, or throw clay at a wall in an acceptable setting.

Inappropriate verbal expressions of anger, e.g., the child calls someone a "no good son of a bitch," can be handled by teaching the child to say, "I am angry," and "You make me mad," instead of insulting the parent or the teacher. It also may be useful to let him go into a special room where he will be alone and let him punch a bag while expressing anger verbally in any manner he chooses. Such a room can be designated the "anger room." This kind of room can also be used for a child to get over his temper tantrums — crying, screaming, stomping, throwing things, etc. He can be told that he can have a tantrum there and can leave when he quiets down. This technique usually works well except in cases where the child is using a tantrum to escape a situation he does not like, e.g., working a puzzle or completing a chore. If he is using temper tantrums to get out of doing something he is supposed to do, and is successful, temper tantrums are being reinforced and may continue.

*Circle a T or an F in Front of Each Statement**

T   F   (1) Accelerator-type reinforcements alone are usually not effective for eliminating undesirable behavior.

T   F   (2) The first two procedures to use to eliminate undesirable behavior in children are to reduce the child's psychobiological deprivation states and pacify him.

T   F   (3) The first two procedures to use to eliminate undesirable behavior in children are to reduce the child's psychobiological deprivation states and to teach him how to deal with frustration.

T   F   (4) The eight psychobiological deprivation states which should be considered when training children are: (a) the need for attention or recognition, (b) the need to satisfy their curiosity, (c) the need for physical
activity, (d) the need to maintain comfortable temperature and humidity levels, (e) the need for bowel and bladder elimination, (f) the need
for food and water, (g) the need to reduce fatigue, and (h) the need to
satisfy the sexual drive.

T   F   (5) It is not necessary to reduce these eight psychobiological deprivation
states in order to eliminate undesirable behavior in children.

T   F   (6) It is necessary to reduce these eight psychobiological deprivation
states in order to eliminate undesirable behavior in children.

T   F   (7) The three steps that should be taken to eliminate frustration problems
are: (a) increase the child's frustration or stress tolerance, (b) eliminate any unreasonable stress to the child, and (c) teach the child an
appropriate way to express his anger.

T   F   (8) Five techniques that can be used to eliminate undesirable behavior
are: (a) extinction, (b) satiation, (c) escape, (d) punishment, and (e)
conditioning incompatible behavior.

T   F   (9) Five techniques that can be used to eliminate undesirable behavior
are: (a) extinction, (b) satiation, (c) avoid setting up the situation that
causes the undesirable behavior, (d) conditioning incompatible behavior, and (e) use of punishment.

Answers are on page 98.

These two procedures, eliminating the child's psychobiological drive
states and teaching him how to deal with frustration, should solve most of
the behavior problems presented by children. In the event that they do not,
then the following five procedures can be used to eliminate undesirable
behavior.

EXTINCTION

Extinction is nothing more than ignoring a child when he does something we do not want him to do. The trainer neither looks at him nor
speaks to him. It is not giving reinforcement. If reinforcement causes
behavior to occur and maintains it, then not giving it should cause it to
diminish and disappear. If a child misbehaves to get attention, e.g., he
smears feces all over the walls of the ward or the home, then if he gets no
attention for it, he may gradually stop doing it. However, there are three
disadvantages to the use of extinction. First, its effects are gradual.
The child may smear feces forty or fifty times after extinction is instituted
before he stops completely. Also, the initial effect of extinction is to make

the undesirable behavior occur more frequently before it begins to deteriorate. Second, ward attendants, parents, and teachers do not always control all reinforcement the child may get for engaging in undesirable behavior. Consider masturbation. It is highly unlikely that masturbation can be eliminated by ignoring it. This very act provides an element of satisfaction or reinforcement, in addition to any reinforcement value the attendant or parent may provide through giving her attention to it. The act of attacking another child may also have reinforcing properties, in addition to any reinforcement the attendant or parent may provide by giving attention. If the attendant or parent does *not* have complete control over the reinforcement that maintains undesirable behavior, the extinction procedure cannot be used effectively. Third, some behavior is so destructive that we cannot afford to let it occur forty or fifty or several hundred times. If extinction was used to eliminate headbanging, the child might be severely brain damaged before he stopped headbanging completely. For these three reasons just cited, extinction may not always be the best technique for eliminating undesirable behavior.

The topic of extinction points out an interesting factor concerned with undesirable behavior. Much undesirable behavior may be unwittingly maintained by parents, teachers, and attendants because they give the child attention when he does such things even though they may scold him when he does it. Being scolded may serve as a reinforcement for a child who gets very little attention otherwise. Headbanging is an example of this kind of behavior. Some children bang their heads against the wall or hit their heads with their hands in order to get attention from attendants or parents. Of course, when they do this, the attendant or parent tells them to stop and often puts them in restraints. But if a child is under enough deprivation for attention, he will misbehave for it. Once he has developed this means of getting attention, he may use it regularly. Some children use this means to "get their way." It is a very effective way to control mothers. This attention can be a powerful reinforcement which the attendant or parent may unknowingly use to maintain a variety of undesirable behaviors, such as soiling and wetting, smearing, breaking out windows, hitting an attendant or mother or other children, etc. By being careful about what kind of behavior she gives attention to, the clever parent or attendant may avoid shaping up new forms of undesirable behavior in children.

*Circle a T or F in Front of Each Statement**

T   F   (1) Extinction is nothing more than *ignoring* a child when he does something we do *not* want him to do.

T   F   (2) Extinction consists of *frowning* and *scolding* a child when he does
            something we do *not* want him to do.
T   F   (3) There are two disadvantages to the use of extinction: (a) its effects
            are gradual and the initial effect of extinction is to make the undesir-
            able behavior occur more frequently before it begins to deteriorate;
            and (b) parents and attendants do *not* always control all reinforcement
            the child may get for engaging in undesirable behavior.
T   F   (4) If an attendant or a parent does not have complete control over all the
            reinforcement that maintains undesirable behavior, she cannot use an
            extinction procedure effectively.

   Answers are on page 98.

SATIATION

   Satiation is the second technique for decelerating or stopping undesirable behavior and has already been considered in the section on psychobiological drive states. Satiation is elimination of deprivation states.
Deprivation not only causes reinforcement to be more effective, it also
causes a child to search around more for reinforcement. A child who is
deprived of attention will not only work harder to get it, but also will do
more different things to obtain it. Some of these things will be in the form
of undesirable behavior. Some children have temper tantrums, pinch and
hit their parents and attendants, smear feces, and get into mother's pots
and pans in the kitchen just to get attention from mother or an attendant.
Even being scolded is reinforcing to them if they are sufficiently deprived
of attention. By giving children attention for desirable behavior, such as
sorting clothes for the laundry, sweeping and mopping floors, making
beds, or running errands for mother or an attendant, their deprivation
states for attention are reduced or they are satiated somewhat. Then they
are less likely to engage in undesirable behavior, particularly if they get
sufficient attention or reinforcement for desirable behavior and no
attention or extinction for undesirable behavior. Attention is a form of
reinforcement.
   Children who are continually getting into mischief are often merely
curious and are simply trying to reduce their *curiosity deprivation state* by
investigating a number of things. If the child has ample opportunity to
satisfy his curiosity in acceptable ways, he will be less likely to get into
mischief of the type that involves investigating. Children who are labeled
hyperactive or *hyperkinetic* usually do not pay attention to other people or
tasks, do not sit still for very long, and always seem to be running about or

jumping up and down. One cause of this kind of behavior is the result of the child's *need for physical activity*. He has a great need to run and jump. By scheduling frequent periods of running and jumping, in the form of planned recreation, as a part of the child's daily schedule, his deprivation for physical activity should be greatly reduced, eliminating one major cause of hyperactivity.

A second satiation procedure can be used to eliminate hoarding. If a child accumulates an excessive amount of certain items, e.g., socks or towels, and keeps them in his clothing or bed or locker or chest of drawers, this habit may be eliminated by providing him with an overabundance of these items. Mr. Leroy Rattitz, building supervisor at Brainerd State Hospital, stopped a retardate from carrying a large number of socks in his shirt by stuffing extra socks in the retardate's shirt each day. After several days of this, the retardate stopped stuffing socks in his shirt.

*Circle a T or F in Front of Each Statement**

T   F   (1) Satiation consists of giving the child all the attention he needs for appropriate behavioi and this in itself may eliminate much undesirable behavior.

T   F   (2) Children who are continually getting into mischief are often doing this to reduce their curiosity deprivation state.

T   F   (3) Curiosity deprivation has nothing to do with a child getting into mischief.

T   F   (4) One way to reduce hyperactivity in children is to reduce their need for physical activity.

T   F   (5) One way to reduce hyperactivity in children is to schedule frequent periods of running and jumping in the form of planned recreation, as part of the child's daily schedule.

T   F   (6) Another satiation procedure, used to eliminate hoarding, is to give the child so much of the thing he craves, that he will no longer hoard it.

T   F   (7) Another satiation procedure, used to eliminate hoarding, is to deprive the child of the thing he craves, until he no longer will hoard it.

Answers are on page 98.

AVOID THE PROVOKING SITUATION

The third way to control undesirable behavior is to simply *avoid the conditions that cause it to occur*. For example, one child on an institutional ward may bully or tease a smaller or less aggressive child until the second child becomes so frustrated that he has a temper tantrum, begins headbanging, or attacks still another child. The way to eliminate undesirable behavior in the second child is to prevent the first child from bullying or teasing him.

*Circle a T or F in Front of the Statement**

T   F   (1) One way to eliminate undesirable behavior is to avoid the condition that causes it to occur, e.g., one child may tease another until he has a temper tantrum. If the first child is prevented from teasing the second, the second child may not have a temper tantrum.

Answer is on page 98.

"THERAPEUTIC" PUNISHMENT AND CONDITIONING INCOMPATIBLE BEHAVIOR

All of the three preceding ways to control undesirable behavior may be effective for reducing it somewhat, but they are not the most effective ways of stopping behavior entirely. The next two techniques, when used together, are most effective for completely eliminating undesirable behavior. These are *conditioning incompatible behavior* and the use of *punishment* in a therapeutic manner. Let us consider conditioning incompatible behavior first. Incompatible behavior is behavior that prevents the undesired behavior from occurring. For example, if you have a child who stutters, the way to eliminate stuttering is to teach him to talk fluently. Fluent speech is incompatible with stuttering. The child can do one or the other, but he cannot do both at the same time. Another example is asking for a cookie. If the child says, "Gimme a cookie," (in a rude tone of voice) and his mother does not like him to ask for it like this and wants to teach him to be polite, she can do so by teaching him to say, "May I please have a cookie." Saying "May I please have a cookie" is incompatible with saying "Gimme a cookie." The child cannot say both at the same time. Incompatible behavior is shaped using a reinforcement procedure. The child is reinforced for making the desired response while either being ignored (extinction) or punished for making the undesired response.

When punishment is used to stop an undesirable response and then an incompatible desirable response is conditioned using reinforcement, one has a very effective means of permanently eliminating undesirable behavior. The term punishment, as used in this manual, refers to a therapeutic treatment procedure as opposed to a vindictive, "old testament" type of discipline technique. For example, a child may break out windows to get attention. Punishment, e.g., restraining the child in a chair for a period of time, could be used to suppress window breaking for attention, and at the same time, the child could be taught a new, more acceptable way to get attention, such as doing chores like sorting clothes, sweeping, or mopping.

Punishment is something which either decelerates or stops behavior. It does not have to hurt the child physically. However, it is usually unpleasant. Hitting a child can be an effective means of punishment, but there are often regulations in schools and institutions that oppose it. Painful electric shock is another effective punishment technique, but this is also a rather controversial procedure which may not be permissible in some institutions or in schools. Sometimes, unusual experiences can serve as effective punishment, e.g., holding a child upside-down or throwing cold water in his face. Restraining a child physically may be an effective punishment technique, particularly if he is being deprived of the opportunity to obtain reinforcement. Holding him tightly in your arms like a baby may also serve as an effective form of punishment for some children. For additional information about decelerating behavior, *see* Azrin and Holz (1966), Browning and Stover (1971), Bucher and Lovaas (1966), Ferster and Perrott (1968), Ferster and Skinner (1957), Gardner (1971), and Reese (1966).

SUMMARY

There are three main procedures that should be used to eliminate undesirable behavior in children. First, the trainer develops a daily program that allows the child to reduce his eight basic psychobiological deprivation states. Second, the child should be taught an appropriate way to express his anger when he is frustrated. Any excessive frustrating conditions, including boredom, should be eliminated and his frustration tolerance level should be increased. Third, in the event that the first two techniques do not eliminate the undesirable behavior, one or more of the five following procedures should be used: extinction, satiation, avoiding the condition that produces the undesirable behavior, conditioning an incompatible response, and punishment.

*Circle a T or F in Front of Each Statement**
T   F   (1) Conditioning incompatible behavior to eliminate undesirable behavior consists of conditioning behavior that keeps the undesirable behavior from occurring.

T   F   (2) The two most effective ways to eliminate undesirable behavior are to use a combination of punishment and satiation.

T   F   (3) The two most effective ways to eliminate undesirable behavior are to use a combination of satiation and conditioning behavior.

T   F   (4) The two most effective ways to eliminate undesirable behavior are to use a combination of punishment and conditioning incompatible behavior.

T   F   (5) Punishment is something which either decelerates or stops behavior: it does not necessarily have to hurt the child physically; however, it is usually unpleasant; punishment is given immediately after the child does something he is not supposed to do.

T   F   (6) Attendants, parents, and teachers sometimes unknowingly maintain undesirable behavior in children by either scolding them or giving them other kinds of attention when they misbehave.

T   F   (7) One way to use a satiation procedure to stop a child from hoarding a particular thing is to give him an excessive amount of the thing he wants until he no longer craves it.

Answers are on page 98.

*Fill in the Missing Words**

(1) Accelerator-type reinforcements alone are usually not very effective for eliminating _____ behavior.

(2) The first two procedures to use to eliminate undesirable behavior in children are to reduce the child's _____ _____ _____ and to teach him how to deal with _____ _____.

(3) It is essential to reduce the eight _____ _____ _____ _____ in order to eliminate undesirable behavior in children.

(4) The three steps that should be taken to eliminate frustration problems in children are: (a) increase the child's _____ _____ _____, (b) eliminate any unreasonable _____ to the child, and (c) teach the child an _____ way to express his _____.

(5) Five techniques that can be used to eliminate undesirable behavior, if the first two cited in question #2 fail, are: (a) _____, (b) _____, (c) _____ _____ _____, (d) _____, and (e) _____ _____ _____ _____ _____ _____ _____.

(6) _____ is nothing more than ignoring a child when he does something we do *not* want him to do.

(7) There are two disadvantages to _____: first, its effects

are _____, and second, ward attendants, teachers and parents do not always control all _____ the child may get for engaging in undesirable behavior.

(8) If an attendant or parent does not have complete control over all the _____ that maintains undesirable behavior, she cannot use an _____ procedure effectively.

(9) _____ consists of giving the child all the attention he needs for appropriate behavior, and this in itself may eliminate much undesirable behavior.

(10) One way to use a _____ procedure to stop a child from hoarding a particular thing is to give him an excessive amount of the thing he wants until he no longer craves it.

(11) One way to eliminate undesirable behavior is to _____ _____ _____ _____ _____ _____ _____, e.g., one child may tease another until he has a temper tantrum. If the first child is prevented from teasing the second, the second child may *not* have a temper tantrum.

(12) _____ _____ _____ to eliminate undesirable behavior consists of conditioning behavior that keeps the undesirable behavior from occurring.

(13) The two most effective ways to eliminate undesirable behavior are _____ and _____ _____ _____.

Answers are on page 99.

*Answer These Questions**
(1) What two procedures should be used first to eliminate undesirable behavior?
(2) What is extinction? How is it used to eliminate undesirable behavior?
(3) What are the two main disadvantages of extinction?
(4) Do attendants, parents, and teachers sometimes unknowingly maintain undesirable behavior in children? How?
(5) What is satiation? How is it used to eliminate undesirable behavior?
(6) Name and describe five ways to eliminate undesirable behavior if the first two procedures are not successful.
(7) Which *two* of these five methods are most effective for eliminating undesirable behavior?

Answers are on page 99.

Answers to T-F, Fill-in, and Essay Questions

T-F on pages 89–90

    (1)   T
    (2)   F
    (3)   T
    (4)   T
    (5)   F
    (6)   T
    (7)   T
    (8)   F
    (9)   T

T-F on pages 91–92

    (1)   T
    (2)   F
    (3)   T
    (4)   T

T-F on page 93

    (1)   T
    (2)   T
    (3)   F
    (4)   T
    (5)   T
    (6)   T
    (7)   F

T-F on page 94

    (1)   T

T-F on pages 95–96

    (1)   T
    (2)   F
    (3)   F
    (4)   T
    (5)   T
    (6)   T
    (7)   T

Fill-in on pages 96–97
- (1) undesirable
- (2) psychobiological deprivation states; frustration
- (3) psychobiological deprivation states
- (4) frustration (or stress) tolerance; stress (or frustration); appropriate; anger
- (5) extinction; satiation; condition incompatible behavior; punishment; and prevent the condition causing the undesirable behavior
- (6) extinction
- (7) extinction; slow; reinforcement
- (8) reinforcement; extinction
- (9) satiation
- (10) satiation
- (11) prevent the condition causing undesirable behavior from occurring
- (12) conditioning incompatible behavior
- (13) punishment and conditioning incompatible behavior

Essay Questions on page 97
- (1) The two procedures that should be used first to eliminate undesirable behavior are: reduce the child's psychobiological deprivation states and teach him to deal with frustration appropriately.
- (2) Extinction is ignoring the child when he engages in undesirable behavior. When the child behaves inappropriately, the trainer ignores him completely.
- (3) The two main disadvantages of extinction are: (a) it is slow and since it frustrates the child, his undesirable behavior usually increases before it decreases; and (b) the trainer must have control over all reinforcement that maintains the undesirable behavior.
- (4) Yes, attendants, parents, and teachers sometimes unknowingly maintain undesirable behavior in children by giving them attention for engaging in undesirable behavior.
- (5) Satiation consists of giving a child all the attention he needs for appropriate behavior, and this in itself may eliminate undesirable behavior. The purpose of a satiation technique is to eliminate deprivation states in children.
- (6) Five ways to eliminate undesirable behavior in children are extinction, satiation, avoid the condition that causes undesirable behavior, condition incompatible behavior, and punishment.
- (7) The two of the five methods that eliminate undesirable behavior most effectively are punishment and conditioning an incompatible response.

CHAPTER 9

Stimulus Control

Shaping and reinforcement principles are used to teach children more behavior and/or new behavior. However, once they have acquired new behavior, it also is important that this behavior occurs under appropriate circumstances. Once a child has been trained to dress himself, he next must be taught *when* and *where* to dress himself, usually in the morning after he has washed and toileted himself on the ward or in the home. If he also has been trained to undress, he needs to be taught the appropriate time and place to undress, usually at toileting time, bathtime, and bedtime on the ward or in the home. In order to train a child to behave appropriately, we have to use a *stimulus control* technique. Stimulus control refers to the fact that certain cues or stimuli in the environment actually control our behavior. Red traffic lights and children running in front of us control our depressing our car's brake pedal when the car is moving. A red traffic light or a child running out in front of our car is an automatic signal to stop. We do not even have to think about it, we just do it. A green traffic light controls our stepping on the accelerator pedal when we are stopped in front of a traffic light on the street. A green traffic light is a signal to go. Speed limit signs control the extent to which we will push down the accelerator pedal as we drive down a street or highway. A toilet controls elimination in most humans, particularly when they are inside buildings. Most people will not eliminate inside buildings unless they are sitting on or standing in front of a toilet in the appropriate state of partial undress. The toilet and lower clothing removed from the genital area are cues that signal the person to eliminate; they actually control elimination.

When a person urinates and defecates only when sitting on or standing in front of a toilet with his or her lower clothing removed, elimination is under *stimulus control* of the toilet and the lower clothing in that particular position as well as bowel and bladder cues. *Stimulus control develops by having a cue become associated with a particular form of behavior that is reinforced.* The reinforcement causes the cues to gain control over the behavior itself. Thus, all behavior is under some kind of stimulus control, and the way to bring behavior under stimulus control is to associate certain stimuli or cues with behavior that is reinforced. By toilet training a child in a bathroom, while he is sitting on a toilet with his pants down and reinforcing defecation or urination, the bathroom, the toilet, and the pants in a lowered position will become cues that control elimination. This may require a number of repetitions before the stimulus control develops effectively.

Many behavioral characteristics which distinguish autistic and retarded children from normal children are due to the child being under inappropriate stimulus control. Autistic children are characterized by not looking at other people when these people speak to them. Their speech, if present, is usually limited to an echolalic or mimicking type or seems to be used for their own amusement, as opposed to being used to communicate with others. When they want to communicate with someone else, e.g., to get someone to give them a toy or food, they usually either lead them by the hand to what they want and point to it, or they have a violent temper tantrum. When they are placed among a group of other children, they usually ignore the other children completely. When they want to express their frustration through anger (the stimulus condition), they often do so by means of self-destructive acts, such as hitting themselves in the face or about the head with their hands or fists and their knees. These are all examples of inappropriate stimulus control. The appropriate response for the child to make when someone calls him by name, is to look them in the eye. The appropriate way to use speech in the presence of others is either to make requests, i.e., ask for things, or to relate experiences. The appropriate way to express anger when frustrated is either to cry quietly in public for a brief period of time, or cry loudly for a long period of time in private, and to expend physical energy by punching a bag or tearing discarded cloth in a room designed for that purpose. The child usually has all of these appropriate behaviors that are necessary for such situations, but he never exhibits them under the proper circumstances.

In order to eliminate such strange or bizarre behavior in an autistic child, we must teach him to behave in other appropriate ways in these situations. We would bring other behaviors under stimulus control of these situations. We would begin by teaching such a child to look at people when they talk to him, i.e., shape attention or eye contact. This is done, of course, by reinforcing the child whenever he looks at the trainer when the trainer calls his name. The trainer may initially have to physically orient the child's head so he is forced to look at him, but by means of contingent reinforcement, can shape up eye contact for increasingly longer periods of time. In time, the child will maintain eye contact for increasingly longer periods of time—if eye contact continues to be contingent upon reinforcement.

Next, the trainer could make food, drink and toys or other things the child likes contingent upon speech in order to shape appropriate speech. At first, the child might only be required to say the name of the thing he wanted. If for example, he wanted juice, he could be required to say "juice" in order to get it. Once he would reliably say "juice," he could be required to say "want juice" and when this verbal expression was well established, he could be required to say, "I want juice." The same contingency could be required for food, snacks, and other things. In addition, echolalia could be punished with "No!" or extinction while appropriate speech was being reinforced.

The child could be trained to relate to or play with other children by initially reinforcing him for giving something to another child and then by reinforcing him for playing simple games with other children. If the child expressed his anger by beating his own head with his hands or fists, he could be physically restrained from headbanging and required to hit the trainer's hand when he wanted to express his anger (in order to teach him an appropriate way to express his anger).

*Circle a T or F in Front of Each Statement**

T   F   (1) A *stimulus control* technique is used to teach a child to behave *appropriately*.

T   F   (2) *Stimulus control* refers to the fact that certain cues or stimuli in the environment actually control one's behavior.

T   F   (3) Stimulus control develops by having a cue become associated with a particular form of behavior that is reinforced.

T   F   (4) Reinforcement is necessary in order for stimulus control to develop.

T   F   (5) If a child soils his pants in the middle of the ward dayroom, elimination is under stimulus control of the ward toilet.

Answers are on page 115.

ESTABLISHING STIMULUS CONTROL

The first attempts that should be made to establish stimulus control over a child after he is enrolled in a training program is to bring eye contact under stimulus control of the child's name. Then other aspects of his behavior would be brought under verbal control by the trainer. As pointed out in Chapter 5, there are three ways to communicate with children: (1) by words or spoken language, (2) by gestures, and (3) by moving the child's body or arms and legs. He may be taught to respond to the verbal commands, "Stand up!", "Sit down!", and "Come here!". At first, the trainer may have to use gestures and physical communication (moving the child's limbs) to get him to respond, but by repeatedly reinforcing the child for correctly following these instructions, the verbal commands themselves usually will acquire control over the behavior. Once the child responds to the verbal commands alone, the physical and gestural forms of communication can be eliminated and the verbal commands alone can be used to control him. When the child responds to the verbal commands alone, i.e., without using gestural and physical cues too, then his behavior is now under stimulus control of the verbal commands to which he is responding. Again, it is the process of getting the child to respond repeatedly in the presence of the commands and reinforcing him for responding appropriately that causes the command to acquire stimulus control over this behavior.

When a child is told by the trainer to take off his shirt or his pants and then is reinforced for doing this, the verbal commands, "Take off your shirt!" or "Take off your pants!", acquire stimulus control over the child taking off his shirt and his pants. Similarly, telling him to put on his shirt and his pants and then reinforcing him for this causes the verbal commands, "Put on your shirt!" and "Put on your pants!", to acquire stimulus control over the child putting on his shirt and his pants. Since language is one important source of stimulus control, if several nurses, attendants, teachers, etc., are working with one child, it is important that they use identical commands given in the same tone of voice, at least early in the program. Once the child learns dressing skills, and his language skills improve, variation in commands may not be so important.

*Circle a T or F in Front of the Statement**

T   F   (1) The three forms of communication one can use to develop stimulus control over a child's behavior are: (a) verbal cues, (b) movement of the child's limbs, and (c) gestures.

Answer is on page 115.

STIMULUS CONTROL PROPERTIES OF THE WARD, THE CLASSROOM, AND THE HOME

Children do not pay attention to everything they hear and see. Hearing and seeing are selective. For this reason, only certain parts or dimensions of the ward, home, and classroom will develop and maintain stimulus control over children. These probably are: (1) the commands or language used by the trainer, (2) the particular person carrying out training, (3) the actual room or location where training is taking place, (4) the location of furniture and other materials in the room where training is taking place, (5) the color of the floor and the walls of the room where training is taking place, (6) the shape of the furniture in the room where training takes place, (7) the time of day when certain events occur, and (8) the sequence of activities that precede the particular behavior of interest. Other dimensions or parts of the ward, home, or classroom probably develop little or no stimulus control over behavior. Although it is not clear to what extent each of these eight conditions acquire stimulus control over behavior, each of them will probably be responsible for behavior occurring appropriately. When a child is taught to dress always in his bedroom, the bedroom itself becomes a stimulus that is controlling dressing. His mother's command, "Get up and get dressed," is also a cue for dressing. The child may learn that when he sees his clothes laid out on his bed, he is to take them off his bed and put them on and to sit in a certain small chair of a specific color and shape to put on his socks and shoes. He may also learn to get dressed around 7:30 in the morning. Thus, the time of day will have stimulus control properties over dressing. Finally, he may also learn to get dressed after he washes his face and hands which is preceded by eliminating in the toilet which in turn is preceded by getting out of bed. The three behaviors, getting out of bed, using the toilet, and washing his face and hands, will also be cues for getting dressed. The same would be true for doing tablework in a classroom or participating in games at recreation time.

*Circle a T or F in Front of Each Statement**

T   F   (1) Once dressing and undressing are worked into the daily routine, certain aspects of the ward or home environment will acquire stimulus control over the child's behavior.

T   F   (2) If the child dresses in the morning after he uses the toilet and bathes, then the order in which these activities occur, as well as the trainer's command, will also develop stimulus control over dressing.

T   F   (3) Physical characteristics of the ward or home itself will also acquire stimulus control over dressing and undressing.

T   F   (4) Physical characteristics of the ward or home will *not* acquire stimulus
control over dressing and undressing in children.

Answers are on page 115.

INFLUENCE OF CHANGE ON STIMULUS CONTROL

Stimulus control is not nearly so stable in retarded and autistic children
as it is in normal children and adults. Sudden changes in the verbal commands used to control specific behavior, in the daily routine or in the
physical characteristics of the ward, home or classroom may disrupt
stimulus control. If this happens, the child will act as if he does not know
what to do, or simply will not behave in a way that is appropriate to that
particular situation. For this reason, it is important to keep these preceding eight conditions as similar as possible and to make any changes in the
ward, home, or classroom environment *gradually* rather than suddenly.
All attendants, parents, and teachers should use identical verbal commands for controlling the child, such as, "Come to me!", "Stand up!",
"Sit down!", "Take off your shirt!", "Put on your shirt!", and "Go to the
toilet!" If everyone uses the same language with the same tone of voice,
the stimulus control properties of these commands over specific behavior
will be greater. If the ward, home, or classroom routine is kept the same
each day and any changes made gradually, such children will probably
behave more appropriately under all circumstances, once they are taught
the behavior that is appropriate for each situation. If the color of the ward,
home, or classroom walls, and the kind and location of furniture is kept
the same or changed only gradually, these children will probably behave
more appropriately under all conditions. If any stimulus changes that must
be made are made *gradually* and *not suddenly*, the child's behavior patterns
that are appropriate to a particular situation are more likely to occur.

An incident that occurred at Columbus State Institute will illustrate
the disruptive effect of a sudden change on stimulus control. We began
a behavior modification project on a ward with the following floor plan.
There were three relatively small bedrooms with adjoining bathrooms,
and one large dayroom. Children were trained to sleep and dress in the
three smaller rooms, and recreational activities, i.e., simple games, were
played in the one large room. Then one day, attendants working the 11:00
p.m. to 7:00 a.m. shift decided that it would be much easier to monitor
the children at night if all of them slept in one large room, the room
used as the recreation room. So, all beds were moved to the one large
room from the three smaller rooms, and the three smaller rooms were

redesignated recreation rooms. This sudden change had a dramatic disruptive effect over the toileting program, the dressing program, and the recreation program. Children who formerly had no elimination accidents began soiling and wetting themselves; they stopped dressing themselves where they formerly were dressing in the morning; and they did little or nothing at recreation time, even though they were playing games well during recreation periods before the room change took place. Many even stopped responding to verbal instructions. It appeared that the change in rooms thoroughly confused them and disrupted all stimulus control.

*Circle a T or F in Front of Each Statement**

T   F   (1) All trainers should use the *same identical commands* when training and maintaining behavior on the ward or in the home so as not to confuse the child and disrupt *stimulus control*.

T   F   (2) It is *not* necessary for trainers to use the *same* identical commands with children in order to avoid disrupting *stimulus control*.

T   F   (3) Sudden changes made in the way furniture is arranged on the ward or in the home will *not* disrupt stimulus control.

T   F   (4) The ward or home routine should be kept the same from day to day in order to maintain *stimulus control*.

T   F   (5) Sudden changes in the ward or home routine will *not* disrupt *stimulus control*.

T   F   (6) *Gradual changes* in the ward or home routine or furniture will *disrupt* stimulus control less than *sudden changes*.

Answers are on page 115.

ATTENTION

Attention is extremely important for establishing stimulus control. A child will neither learn nor have stimulus control develop over his behavior if he is not paying attention to the cues being used to try to control him. Gestures are useless for controlling children if they are not looking at the trainer and paying attention to her at the time she gives them. Not only should the trainer be sure that the child is paying attention to her when she is trying to teach him something, but she should also be sure he is attending to exactly what she wants him to. Retarded and autistic children are not sensitive to all of the subtle cues in their environment that normal children are. Therefore, trainers should put a lot of emphasis into their verbal commands, use exaggerated, rather dramatic gestures, and reinforce children verbally with considerable enthusiasm. It is also important to keep the child's attention focused on the problem of interest when training him.

Because these children are not paying attention to all aspects of their physical environment, it may be possible to change certain parts of the ward or home and not disrupt stimulus control. However, if other characteristics of the ward or home are changed this may produce a disruptive effect on their behavior. Color, shape, and position are probably the most important cues for retardates. They probably pay more attention to these cues than others. Thus, if these characteristics are changed, stimulus control may be disrupted rather dramatically since they pay attention to these cues, and these cues control appropriate behavior. Rearranging the furniture on the ward or home, replacing old furniture with new furniture that looks quite different, or changing the paint on the walls from yellow to blue, may disrupt their behavior considerably since these parts of the room may be the cues that maintain stimulus control.

Circle a T or F in Front of Each Statement*

T   F   (1) If a child is *not* paying *attention*, it will *not* be possible to develop stimulus control over his behavior.

T   F   (2) Since children do *not* pay *attention* to *all* parts of their environment, it is possible to change some stimuli without disrupting stimulus control.

T   F   (3) A trainer should use *exaggerated, dramatic commands and gestures* when training a child in order to insure that the child understands him.

T   F   (4) The *shape* of furniture and other parts of the ward or home can be an important source of *stimulus control*.

T   F   (5) The color of furniture and walls of the home or ward can be an important source of *stimulus control*.

*Answers are on page 115.

FADING AND PROMPTING

Because sudden change exerts such a disruptive effect over stimulus control, and because it is so important to keep the child's attention focused on the task at hand, we need a special procedure to maintain stimulus control under changing stimulus conditions. This technique is a combination of *fading* and *prompting*. Let us consider fading first. *Fading is the act of gradually changing cues in the child's environment.* If we introduce new cues and do it in a gradual manner, we are *fading in cues.* If we take away cues and do it gradually, we are *fading out cues.* For example, if we use physical movements of the child's limbs, gestures, and a ver-

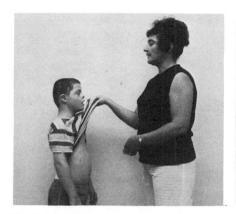

Fig. 9.1-1 The trainer uses a verbal command and a physical prompt to communicate with the child.

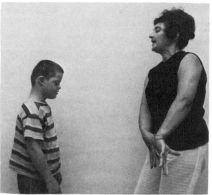

Fig. 9.1-2 The trainer uses a verbal command and a gesture to communicate with the child.

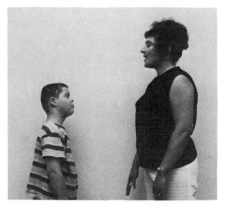

Fig. 9.1-3 The trainer uses a verbal command alone to communicate with the child.

bal command, "Take off your shirt," to get a child to take off a pullover shirt, and then gradually eliminate movement of the child's limbs, gestures, and leave only the verbal command, we are *fading out* movement of the limbs and fading out gestures. This procedure is illustrated in Fig. 9.1. In Fig. 9.1-1, the trainer is using the verbal command, "Take off your shirt," accompanied by a physical prompt, pulling upward on the shirt. In Fig. 9.1-2, the trainer is no longer using the physical prompt but is still using the verbal command accompanied by gestures. Finally, in Fig.

9.1-3, gestures have also been faded out and the child is taking off his shirt for the verbal command alone. If gestures and movement of the limbs are removed too soon, dressing behavior may be disrupted. If this happens, the trainer should reintroduce gestures to reestablish stimulus control, and if the child still does not put on his shirt, movement of the limbs also should be reestablished. Then fading procedures should be repeated after dressing behavior stabilizes.

Prompting consists of giving children special cues that direct their attention toward the task the trainer is attempting to teach them. These cues usually consist of physical manipulation of some part of the child's body, although gestural and verbal prompts are also used. The purpose of a prompt is to make it clear to a child what he is supposed to do. For example, a speech therapist may be attempting to teach a child with protruding front teeth to say ball, as illustrated in Fig. 9.2. Because the child has this protrusion, he finds it is difficult to press his lips together to make a "ba" sound. Since he cannot put his lips together, he ends up saying "all" when he tries to say "ball." In order to help him press his lips together, the therapist uses a physical prompt, as shown in Fig. 9.2-1. She presses his lips together between her thumb and forefinger, and says, "Say ball." The child begins to generate the sound, and when the therapist lets go of his lips, he says, "ball." Once the vocal response "ball" is well established under these conditions, the therapist *fades out her* physical prompt and *fades in a physical prompt controlled by the child* (*see* Fig. 9.2-2). The child presses his own lips together between his thumb and

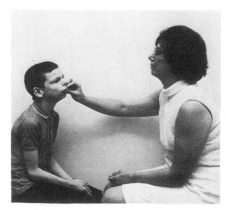

Fig. 9.2-1 The therapist presses the child's lips between her thumb and forefinger.

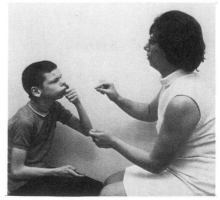

Fig. 9.2-2 The child presses his own lips together between his thumb and forefinger.

forefinger, begins to produce the sound, releases his lips, and produces the sound "ball." After this response is well established, the child *fades out* his own physical prompt and says "ball" without using his fingers to close his lips. If the behavior is lost after a prompt is faded out, it should be reinstituted and perhaps be withdrawn more gradually next time. Sometimes, physical prompts may have to be withdrawn and reinstituted several times before the behavior is well established.

A second example of the use of physical prompts is the case where a child is being taught to take off a dress. We often find it helpful to take her hand, pull it down behind her back, make it grip the dress itself, and then pull the arm upward as we say, "Take off your dress." Once this type of prompt has undressing behavior under control, we may fade out the physical prompt and use a gestural prompt paired with the verbal command, "Take off your dress," where we motion to the child to take off her dress. After the behavior is well established, we would fade out the gestural prompt and simply use a verbal command alone, i.e., "Take off your dress."

If a child is halfway through taking off or putting on a garment and runs into difficulty, we would use either a physical, a gestural, or a verbal prompt to keep her moving. If she had pulled her dress down over her head but failed to put her arms in the sleeves, we would gently push an elbow upward (physical prompt) and say, "Come on now, put on your dress." Or we could just use a gestural prompt if she were far enough along in training so that the physical prompt was unnecessary. Finally, some children appear to tire out halfway through taking off or putting on a garment during training. They just stop. It is often sufficient simply to "hustle" them along with words, e.g., "Come on now, let's get that dress off; Come on, take off your dress; Let's go now."

*Circle a T or F in Front of Each Statement**

T   F   (1) *Fading* stimuli consists of changing stimuli *gradually* so as not to disrupt stimulus control.

T   F   (2) If we introduce new cues and do it gradually, we are *fading in cues*.

T   F   (3) If we take away cues in a gradual manner, we are *fading out cues*.

T   F   (4) *Prompting* consists of giving children special cues that will direct their attention toward the task the trainer is attempting to teach them.

T   F   (5) The purpose of a *prompt* is to make it clear to a child what it is he is supposed to do.

T   F   (6) If a trainer presses a child's lips together between her thumb and forefinger in order to help him make a "ba" sound, she is using a *physical prompt*.

Answers are on pages 115–116.

GETTING BEHAVIOR TO OCCUR IN NEW SITUATIONS

This problem of stimulus control becomes very important when we are teaching a child to behave appropriately on the ward or in the home or in one particular situation, and we also want him to behave appropriately in other situations, such as the classroom, a vocational workshop, or a recreational room. For example, we usually toilet train a child in his own home or on his own ward, but we also want him to be able to use the toilet in the bathroom at school, at the workshop, and at the recreation center. He may not eliminate in the toilets in these new places without specific training, since the location of the bathrooms in these new places is different from the bathrooms at home or on the ward, and since the physical characteristics of these new bathrooms will probably differ from those where he was originally trained. The bathroom walls may be of a different color, the toilets and wash basins may look different or be located differently in the bathroom. For this reason, these children will probably need supplemental toilet training. They will need to learn to get up and walk to the bathroom when the teacher or supervisor tells them to, they will have to learn how to find the bathroom, they will have to use the toilet appropriately after they get into the bathroom, and they will have to find their way back to the classroom, recreation room, or workshop area.

Similar problems will probably occur if the child is in school or in the workshop at lunchtime. He will have to be trained how to carry out the lunchtime routine that is appropriate to the school or workshop. These same problems may occur if the child is introduced to clothes that are different from those he has learned to take off and put on. If buttons on new clothing are smaller, sewed on tighter, or are harder to get through the buttonholes, the child may require supplementary buttoning training. The same problem would probably exist if the child was trained to put on loafer or slipper type shoes and then was introduced to lace-up shoes, or if he had been trained to put on boxer short-waistband type pants and then was introduced to pants with a fly. The top buttons on the flies of some pants are harder to button than others. This problem, too, would require special training.

Similar problems can also occur with undesirable behavior. A child can be trained *not* to have temper tantrums at home in the presence of his mother, but still may have them when he begins to go to school. Since mother and the physical characteristics of the home are maintaining stimulus control over *not* having temper tantrums, or over behavior that is incompatible with temper tantrums, once he goes to school, stimulus control is not present in this new situation (the classroom), nor is it maintained by this new person (the teacher). For this reason, the teacher may have to reinstitute the same procedures used previously to eliminate temper tantrums. However, it probably will not take her as long to bring temper tantrums under control as it did mother, since this problem was dealt with before, and there should be some carryover to the new situation. There should be some transfer of training. For additional information about stimulus control, *see* Browning and Stover (1971), Ferster and Perrott (1968), Gardner (1971), Lovaas (1969), Reese (1966), Sidman and Stoddard (1967), Terrace (1966), Trabasso and Bower (1968), Watson (1970), and Zeaman (1963).

*Circle a T or F in Front of the Statement**
T   F   (1) A child who is toilet trained on his home ward or in his home may also have to receive toilet training in other parts of the institution or school if he is to use these other toilets in other parts of the institution or school.

Answer is on page 116.

SUMMARY

New behavior is taught using *shaping* and *reinforcement* procedures, but behavior is conditioned to occur appropriately through the use of *stimulus control* and *reinforcement* techniques. Stimulus control means that certain stimuli in one's environment control his behavior. Because stimulus control is rather unstable in retarded and autistic children, any changes in the home or ward environment should be made gradually. All trainers should use identical commands with such children, the ward or home routine should be kept fairly constant, and changes in the location and type of furniture or the color of the walls on the ward or in the home should be made gradually. Because neither learning nor stimulus control will develop if the child is not paying attention to the trainer, it is important to ascertain that he is attending to particular stimuli being used by the trainer. *Prompting* and *fading* techniques will help to direct the child's attention properly during training. If the trainer is attempting to develop verbal stimulus control over certain behavior, she should emphasize her gestures and words to ensure that the child attends to them. In order to make certain that appropriate behavior will also occur in new situations, supplemental training should be given in the classroom, recreational area, or workshop after the child is introduced to these new places.

*Fill in the Missing Words**

(1) A stimulus control technique is used to teach a child to behave _____ _____.

(2) _____ _____ refers to the fact that certain cues or stimuli in the environment actually control one's behavior.

(3) Stimulus control develops by having a cue become associated with a particular form of behavior that is _____.

(4) _____ is necessary in order for stimulus control to develop.

(5) The three forms of communication one can use to develop stimulus control over a child's behavior are: (a) _____, (b) _____ _____ _____ _____ _____, and (c) _____.

(6) All trainers should use the same identical _____ when training and maintaining behavior on the ward or in the home so as *not* to confuse the child and disrupt _____ _____.

(7) The ward or home routine should be kept the _____ from day to day in order to maintain _____ _____.

(8) _____ changes in the ward or home routine will disrupt _____ _____.

(9) _____ changes in the ward or home routine or furniture will disrupt stimulus control less than _____ changes.

(10) *Fading* stimuli consists of _____ changing stimuli so as *not* to disrupt stimulus control.

(11) If a child is not paying _____ it will *not* be possible to develop stimulus control.

(12) Since children do not pay _____ to *all* parts of their environment, it is possible to change some stimuli without disrupting stimulus control.

(13) A trainer should use exaggerated, dramatic _____ and _____ when training such a child in order to ensure that the child understands her.

(14) The _____, _____, and _____ of furniture and other parts of the ward can be an important source of *stimulus control.*

Answers are on page 116.

*Answer These Questions**

(1) What is stimulus control?
(2) How does stimulus control develop?
(3) What is the importance of reinforcement for developing stimulus control?
(4) Why is it important to bring behavior under stimulus control?

(5) What three forms of communication can be used to develop stimulus control over a child's behavior?

(6) Why is it important for all trainers to use the same identical commands and gestures when training and controlling these children?

(7) Why is it important not to make sudden changes in the ward or home environment such as moving furniture around?

(8) Why should the ward or home routine be kept the same from day to day?

(9) Why should any changes in ward or home conditions be made *gradually* rather than *suddenly*?

(10) What is *fading*?

(11) What would probably happen if a child who was toilet trained on his home ward was transferred to another ward that had a bathroom that was located in a part of the ward different from the home ward and that was physically quite different from the bathroom on the home ward?

(12) What is the importance of getting the child's *attention* before trying to train him?

(13) Why should a trainer use exaggerated, dramatic commands and gestures when training these children?

Answers are on pages 116–117.

Answers to T-F, Fill-in, and Essay Questions

T-F on page 102
      (1)   T
      (2)   T
      (3)   T
      (4)   T
      (5)   F

T-F on page 103
      (1)   T

T-F on pages 104–105
      (1)   T
      (2)   T
      (3)   T
      (4)   F

T-F on page 106
      (1)   T
      (2)   F
      (3)   F
      (4)   T
      (5)   F
      (6)   T

T-F on page 107
      (1)   T
      (2)   T
      (3)   T
      (4)   T
      (5)   T

T-F on page 110
      (1)   T
      (2)   T
      (3)   T
      (4)   T

(5)   T
(6)   T

T-F on page 112
   (1)   T

Fill-in on page 113
   (1)   appropriately
   (2)   stimulus control
   (3)   reinforced
   (4)   reinforcement
   (5)   gestures; movement of the limbs; and words
   (6)   commands; stimulus control
   (7)   same; stimulus control
   (8)   sudden; stimulus control
   (9)   gradual; sudden
   (10) gradually
   (11) attention
   (12) attention
   (13) commands; gestures
   (14) color; shape; and location

Essay Questions on pages 113–114
   (1)   Stimulus control refers to the fact that certain cues or stimuli in the environment actually control one's behavior.
   (2)   Stimulus control develops by having a cue become associated with a particular form of behavior that is reinforced.
   (3)   Stimulus control will not develop without reinforcement.
   (4)   It is important to bring behavior under stimulus control so that it will occur appropriately.
   (5)   The three forms of communication are words, gestures, and movement of the child's body or arms and legs.
   (6)   It is important for all trainers to use identical commands and gestures during training in order to maintain stimulus control and *not* confuse the child.
   (7)   Sudden changes in the ward or home environment can disrupt stimulus control.
   (8)   If the ward or home routine are changed suddenly rather than being kept the same, stimulus control may be disrupted.
   (9)   When changes are made gradually rather than suddenly, stimulus control usually is not disrupted.
   (10) Fading is gradually changing the cues that control behavior.
   (11) The child would begin having toileting accidents.

(12) Children do not learn if they are not paying attention.
(13) Trainers should use exaggerated, dramatic commands and gestures during training to ensure that the child pays attention, understands what he is to do, and stimulus control is maintained.

CHAPTER 10

Data Collection

If a behavior modification project is to be effective, some form of relatively objective evaluation system should be used to determine the influence of treatment on the child. An objective evaluation or record keeping system is needed for three reasons: first, merely observing the child and using your memory to recall whether he is getting better, worse, or is remaining the same can be very deceptive. Our memories distort and we tend to remember what we want to remember. If we want the child to get better, we will tend to remember events that indicate to us he is improving, and forget those that indicate he is not making progress. Second, if the child stops making progress in the training project, and we become discouraged, we tend to forget the extent to which he had been making progress before. An objective evaluation or record keeping system tends to keep us "reality oriented" or honest with ourselves. Third, after a child has been in a training project for six months to a year, memories become dim, and trainers forget the course of total progress since the beginning of the treatment program. *Without an objective evaluation or record keeping system, we cannot accurately and reliably determine progress made by the child in the training project.*

More specifically, an objective data system serves two important functions: first, it makes it possible to determine whether children in the program are changing, and the direction and extent of change. Second, it allows one to assess the relationship between different programs within the overall training project, e.g., self-help, social, vocational education, and language, and the kinds of changes each of these programs are producing.

There are four types of data recording techniques that will be reviewed in this chapter: (1) frequency, (2) duration, (3) quality, and (4) diagnosis.

Circle a T or F in Front of Each Statement*

T   F   (1) Data collection systems are needed in a training program so that we can accurately and reliably determine whether the child is getting better or worse or is making no progress at all.

T   F   (2) Data collection systems are *not* necessary for determining the progress made by a child in a training program.

T   F   (3) Without an objective data system, we cannot accurately and reliably determine progress made by the child in the training program.

*Answers are on page 139.

FREQUENCY

A Frequency Data Recording Procedure is the simplest type of data recording technique. It is nothing more than a *tally system.* The trainer simply makes a mark on a piece of paper each time a response occurs. Figure 10.1 illustrates this type of recording technique. Notice at the top of the page, the data sheet has blanks for the type of program (in this example, *Toileting*), the name of the child, the name of the trainer, and the type of response being recorded (in this example, *Elimination*). Then, there is a place to put a total score if one is available, a place to put the date, the session number (the number of days the child has been in this particular program), and the length of the session or the recording period each day. There also is a *score key* which indicates to the trainer how the response of interest should be recorded. Finally, there is a section for remarks at the bottom of the page that allows the trainer to write brief interpretations about the behavior that is occurring. The two classes of responses being recorded in Fig. 10.1 are accidents (soiling and wetting) and appropriate elimination (urination and defecation in the toilet). If the child has an accident during the observation period covered by this data sheet, the trainer makes a tally mark on the line designated *Soiled* and *Wet*. If the child eliminates in the toilet, the trainer makes a tally mark on the line designated *Urination* and *Defecation*. At the end of the observation period, the tally marks are added up for each category yielding a total score for that day.

The data recording procedure illustrated in Fig. 10.1 is the simplest type of frequency data recording technique and can be used to record behaviors like bowel and bladder elimination. It can also be used to record

FREQUENCY DATA SHEET

TYPE OF PROGRAM *TOILETING*   SCORE *3Sw/8 UD*
PATIENT *BILLY SMITH*   DATE *9/25/70*
TRAINER *MARY SMITH*   SESSION NUMBER *4*
TYPE OF RESPONSE *ELIMINATION*   SESSION LENGTH *24 hrs.*

SCORE KEY: PUT A TALLY MARK FOR EACH RESPONSE
OBSERVED, E.G., 1111

TASK OR RESPONSE	FREQUENCY
SOILED + WET	III
URINATION +	*卌 III*
DEFECATION	

REMARKS: *Billy had to be prompted to use the toilet 5 out of 8 times. He used the toilet independently 3 times.*

Fig. 10.1   Example of a Frequency Data Sheet that utilizes only a tally mark.

aggressive behavior, where one child attacks another by hitting, pinching, or biting him, or by calling the other child names. Finally, it can be used to record how often a child jumps up from his seat during a class period or how often he has temper tantrums each day.

Figure 10.2 illustrates how this form of frequency data system would be used to record aggressive behavior. The first step before actually recording aggressive behavior is to clearly identify the types of behaviors that will be classified as aggressive. In this example, they are hitting, biting, and shoving. The behaviors being recorded should be specified so that

FREQUENCY DATA SHEET

TYPE OF PROGRAM *AGGRESSIVNESS*   SCORE *H6/83/52*
PATIENT *BILLY SMITH*   DATE *9/25/70*
TRAINER *MARY BROWN*   SESSION NUMBER *8*
TYPE OF RESPONSE *ATTACKING*   SESSION LENGTH_____

SCORE KEY: PUT A TALLY MARK FOR EACH RESPONSE
             OBSERVED, E.G., 1111

TASK OR RESPONSE	FREQUENCY
HITTING	HHL I
BITING	III
SHOVING	II

REMARKS: *Billy seems to attack other children after he becomes frustrated. This usually happens when he is told to do a difficult task.*

Fig. 10.2   Example of a Frequency Data Sheet used to record aggressive behavior.

they are clear to all concerned with training that particular child. Any member of the group watching the child being aggressive should be able to agree with everyone else working with the child that he did, in fact, hit, bite, or shove someone when other members of the group reported he did. This problem refers, of course, to clearly identifying the *target behaviors* that are to be eliminated. When target behaviors are clearly specified, a group of persons who are independently observing a child engaging in aggressive behavior will be able to agree among themselves each time a hitting, biting, or shoving response occurs. Although this type of frequency recording system is very simple and easy to carry out, it is of limited value because it provides limited information. It only indicates the total number of responses in a broad class that occurs in a given period of time. With slight modifications, however, a frequency data system can be extremely useful.

Two ways to increase the value of a Frequency Data Recording Procedure and still keep it relatively simple are to substitute a coded letter for a tally mark and also record the time when the response occurred. Substitution of a coded letter is illustrated in Fig. 10.3. Instead of a tally mark, one of four letters would be used to indicate each time an elimination response occurred. "U" stands for urinate, "D" for defecate, "W" for wet, and "S" for soil. The coded letter not only indicates that an elimination re-

FREQUENCY DATA SHEET

TYPE OF PROGRAM _TOILETING_   SCORE_____
PATIENT _DONNY   BROOK_   DATE _9/25/70_
TRAINER _MARY   HELSONBRU_ SESSION NUMBER __9__
TYPE OF RESPONSE _ELIMINATION_   SESSION LENGTH_____

SCORE KEY: PUT A TALLY MARK FOR EACH RESPONSE
            OBSERVED, E.G., 1111 —— Code with
            U = URINATE, D = DEFECATE,
            S = SOILED , + W = WET

TASK OR RESPONSE	FREQUENCY
ELIMINATION	U U U D W W W S U U U

REMARKS:
Donny appears to wet himself when he shivers.

Fig. 10.3 Example of a Frequency Data Sheet with a coded letter substituted for a tally mark.

sponse occurred, but also shows the type of elimination response. No more time is required to use this slight modification in the frequency data system than a tally mark, and additional valuable information is provided.

Recording the time the response occurred transforms the frequency data system into an even more useful instrument. As illustrated in Fig. 10.4, each time a response occurs, the trainer uses a coded letter to record the type of response and then records the time the response occurred beside the coded letter. This is the type of data system used in our Columbus State Institute Ward Behavior Modification Project to determine elimination operant levels for our toileting program. By recording both the type of elimination response and the time it occurred, we quickly can

FREQUENCY DATA SHEET

TYPE OF PROGRAM _TOILETING_ SCORE____
PATIENT _BENNY BRUN_ DATE _9/33/72_
TRAINER _ELSA H ESOUA_ SESSION NUMBER _4_
TYPE OF RESPONSE _ELIMINATION_ SESSION LENGTH____

SCORE KEY: PUT A TALLY MARK FOR EACH RESPONSE
OBSERVED, E.G., 1111 — — CODE WITH TIME;
U = URINATE, D = DEFECATE, S = SOIL +
W = WET

TASK OR RESPONSE	FREQUENCY
ELIMINATION	U 6:15AM, D 7:05AM, U8:30AM, W 10:15AM, U 1150 AM

REMARKS: This is the 3rd straight day Benny has D at 7:05 AM

Fig. 10.4 Example of a Frequency Data Sheet with a coded letter and a time entry substituted for a tally mark.

determine the child's elimination habit pattern. We also used this same data system to record progress made in our toileting program.

If a single trainer is working with a large number of children in a toilet training program such as a ward situation, the data recording system illustrated in Fig. 10.4 may become too time consuming. One way to simplify it is to make up data sheets with blocks of time bracketed off, as illustrated in Fig. 10.5. In this data sheet, the child's entire waking day is broken down into one-hour blocks, beginning with six in the morning and terminating at nine in the evening. If the child eliminates during the day, the trainer simply puts the appropriate coded letter in the correct time slot (notice the code key in the lower left corner of the data sheet). For example, if the child urinated at 9:15 a.m., a "U" would be placed in the 9–10 time block. If he soiled himself at 11:45 a.m., an "S" would be placed in the 11–12 time block. There are fourteen date entries on this data sheet, so it can be used for a two-week period.

*Circle a T or F in Front of Each Statement**

T   F   (1) A Frequency Data Recording Procedure is the most complicated type of data system.

T   F   (2) A Frequency Data Recording Procedure utilizes a tally technique.

T   F   (3) By substituting a coded letter for a tally mark and adding a time entry, the Frequency Data Recording Procedure provides a highly useful technique for evaluating a toilet training program.

T   F   (4) By incorporating a graded score, e.g., 0–4 or A–D, the Frequency Data Recording Procedure becomes a useful procedure for evaluating aggressive behavior.

T   F   (5) A Frequency Data Recording Procedure can be used to record bowel and bladder elimination, aggressive behavior, temper tantrums, and "hyperactivity," e.g., a child repeatedly jumps up from his seat at a table in a classroom.

Answers are on page 139.

DURATION

All behavior is not suited to a frequency-type recording system. Some behavior is more usefully described in terms of duration or time. Sometimes we want to know *how long the behavior lasted or how long it has been since the behavior occurred.* A Duration Data System is used to make this type of record. It provides us with all the information that a Frequency Data Recording System does (since each time entry is equivalent to a tally mark and indicates one behavioral occurrence) plus includ-

Name	Date	Hours 6AM – 9PM	6-7	7-8	8-9	9-10	10-11	11-12	12-1	1-2	2-3	3-4	4-5	5-6	6-7	7-8	8-9
Billy Doyle	9/13/70		W			U		S	U		U		D		W		U

D – Defecate
U – Urinate
S – Soil
W – Wet

Fig. 10.5 Example of a Frequency Data Sheet with blocks of time bracketed off.

125

ing information about the time or duration element. We find such a system useful for recording how long a temper tantrum lasted or how long it has been since a child had a temper tantrum. We may want to know how long a child is sitting in his seat and working at a task without jumping up or how long a child sat still at storytime (without fidgeting) in a preschool program. Such behavior is best measured by a Duration Data Recording Procedure. Examples of this type of recording procedure are given in Figs. 10.6 and 10.7. Figure 10.6 illustrates how the Duration Data Recording Procedure would be used to record the length of time that a child will sit at a table uninterrupted. Since there was only one opportunity each day for the child to work at developing uninterrupted sitting

DURATION DATA SHEET

TYPE OF PROGRAM *SITTING AT TABLE* SCORE_____

PATIENT *MARY HAWKINS*   DATE ~~_____~~ *9/2 —*

TRAINER *MARIA ONGNARO*   SESSION NUMBER *5—14*

TYPE OF RESPONSE *SITTING UNINTER.* SESSION LENGTH *50 MIN*

SCORE KEY: ENTER ~~TIME RESPONSE BEGAN FOLLOWED BY~~
~~DURATION OF RESPONSE, E.G., 12:33PM 12'15"~~
TIME CHILD SPENT SITTING WITHOUT JUMPING UP

RESPONSE	DURATION
UNINTERRUPTED SITTING	
9/2/70	10 MIN
9/3/70	14 MIN
9/4/70	17 MIN
9/5/70	24 MIN
9/6/70	30 MIN
9/9/70	42 MIN
9/9/70	35 MIN
9/10/70	44 MIN
9/11/70	50 MIN
9/12/70	50 MIN

REMARKS:

ON 9/9/70 Mary appeared to be very agitated and uncomfortable; I sent her to the nurse and found she had a fever

Fig. 10.6   Example of application of Duration Data Sheet to record uninterrupted sitting.

behavior, each entry on the data sheet represents a different day. Dates are recorded in the left hand margin.

Figure 10.7 illustrates an application of the Duration Recording Procedure in which two measures are being used: (1) how long the child engaged in the behavior, and (2) how long since the behavior last occurred. In this example, the behavior of interest was headbanging. The first entry made is the time the behavior occurred and the second entry indicates how long the behavior lasted. By determining the periods of time between time entries, we have an indication of the time that elapsed between occurrences of the behavior. Both kinds of information are useful for assessing progress made in a headbanging treatment program. This type of data recording procedure would provide more useful information about

DURATION DATA SHEET

TYPE OF PROGRAM *ELIM. OF HEADBNG* SCORE_____
PATIENT *BILLY MINALO* DATE *9/2/70*
TRAINER *MARY DESERVO* SESSION NUMBER *4*
TYPE OF RESPONSE *NO HEADBANG* SESSION LENGTH *24 hrs.*

SCORE KEY: ENTER TIME RESPONSE BEGAN FOLLOWED BY
DURATION OF RESPONSE, E.G., 12:33PM--12'15"

RESPONSE	DURATION
TIME BET/ HDBNG	6:15 AM -- 2'12", 10:30 AM -- 1'48", 11:05 AM -- 55", 4:15 PM -- 1'28", 9:54 PM -- 3'42"

REMARKS: *Billy seems to HBng when he gets frustrated*

Fig. 10.7 Example of Duration Data Sheet where both time of occurrence and duration entries are used.

a behavior such as headbanging than a Frequency Data Recording Procedure.

*Circle a T or F in Front of Each Statement**

T F (1) All behavior can be conveniently recorded using a Frequency Data Recording Procedure.

T F (2) A Duration Data Recording Procedure is needed to record how long behavior lasted or how long it has been since behavior occurred.

T F (3) ·A Duration Data Recording Procedure would probably be more useful to evaluate a program designed to eliminate headbanging than a Frequency Data Recording Procedure.

Answers are on page 139.

QUALITATIVE

A third type of data recording procedure is the Qualitative Data Recording Procedure. This recording procedure not only provides the same information as the Frequency Procedure, but also *grades the response*. As illustrated in Fig. 10.8, grades can be of the form 0, 1, 2, 3, 4 or they could be A, B, C, D. The child performs a task and receives a grade on that task. In Fig. 10.8, the child attempted to put the three-piece puzzle together eight times and the five-piece puzzle eight times, and received a grade each time he tried to put it together. Since our own programs are concerned with extremely negativistic children, we give a grade of 0 to a child who does not respond or refuses to respond, a grade of 1 if he attempts the task but is clearly incorrect, a grade of 2 for a poor approximation, a grade of 3 for a good approximation, and a grade of 4 for an excellent approximation to the desired target behavior.

It is important that a group of persons working with a child on this type of task will agree among themselves on the grade given for a particular response or attempted task solution. In order to ensure a high degree of agreement between trainers on the grade given, clearcut rules should be established concerning what constitutes justification for a grade of 0, 1, 2, 3, and 4. Using the three-piece puzzle in Fig. 10.8 as an illustration, a group of trainers might agree that the child would get a grade of 0 only if he did not respond when told to put the three-piece formboard puzzle together. They might agree that he would get a grade of 1 if he tried to assemble the puzzle, but failed to put a single piece in its proper place. A grade of 2 might be given if the child put all three pieces in their proper places, but he had to try putting each piece in several places before he

QUALITATIVE DATA SHEET

TYPE OF PROGRAM _PUZZLES-EDUC_ SCORE_____
PATIENT_BILLY BROWN_____ DATE_9/4/70_
TRAINER_BETTY SMITH_____ SESSION NUMBER _5_
TYPE OF RESPONSE _COMPLETING_ SESSION LENGTH_____
                    PUZZLES

SCORE KEY: 0 = NO RESPONSE
            1 = INCORRECT RESPONSE
            2 = POOR APPROXIMATION
            3 = GOOD APPROXIMATION
            4 = EXCELLENT APPROXIMATION

TASK											
3-PIECE PUZZLE	1	2	3	2	4	3	4	4			
5-PIECE PUZZLE	1	1	2	2	2	2	3	3			

REMARKS:

Fig. 10.8 Example of a Qualitative Data Sheet used to record preschool curriculum type performance.

found the correct location for that piece. The child might receive a grade of 3 if he put two of the three pieces in their correct positions the first time he attempted them, but placed one piece in an incorrect place one time before he found the correct location. A grade of 4 might be given if the child put all three pieces of the puzzle in their correct positions the first time he tried each one.

The Qualitative Data Recording Procedure is useful for recording performance in educational programs (as illustrated in Fig. 10.8), language programs, social behavior programs, vocational programs, and self-help skill programs. An example of the way it might be used in a language program is illustrated in Fig. 10.9. The example refers to the Echoic Speech Development phase of our language program at Columbus State

QUALITATIVE DATA SHEET

TYPE OF PROGRAM *ECHOIC — SPEECH*   SCORE_____
PATIENT *DON DOMO*   DATE *9/14/71*
TRAINER *MARY NEFFORONI*   SESSION NUMBER *4*
TYPE OF RESPONSE *WORD PRODUCTION* SESSION LENGTH____

SCORE KEY: 0 = NO RESPONSE
            1 = INCORRECT RESPONSE
            2 = POOR APPROXIMATION
            3 = GOOD APPROXIMATION
            4 = EXCELLENT APPROXIMATION

TASK										
BALL	3	4	3	4	4	4	4	4		
BOOK	2	3	2	4	3	4	3	3		
BED	2	3	4	3	3	4	3	3		
BABY	0	0	1	2	2	2	3	2		

REMARKS:

Fig. 10.9 Example of a Qualitative Data Sheet used to record performance in a language program.

Institute. The child is receiving speech production training on four words: ball, book, bed, and baby. If he makes no vocal response at all when the therapist instructs him, "Say ball," he gets a grade of 0. If he makes a sound, but it is unintelligible, he gets a grade of 1. If he makes a sound that can be identified by the listener as ball, but is a poor approximation, he gets a grade of 2. If the child says "ball" and vocalizes it fairly clearly, he receives a grade of 3. If he says "ball" and says it quite clearly, he gets a grade of 4. Again, the grading system should be such that everyone involved in the language program would agree on the grade given for each vocal response made by a child in training, if they were all there at the same time grading him independently.

When programs are developed for teaching children educational, language, social, and self-help skills, *criteria should be established for advancing the child through various steps of the program.* Trainers need to establish a rule concerning when the child should progress from step 1 in a program to step 2, from step 2 to step 3, from step 3 to step 4, etc. The purpose of the criterion is to ensure that the child does not move on from one step in the program to the next too soon, i.e., before he is ready to, but also moves from step to step as quickly as possible. Figure 10.10 illustrates the use of a criterion. This figure illustrates training a child in a

QUALITATIVE DATA SHEET

TYPE OF PROGRAM *BEAD STRINGING* SCORE_____
PATIENT *JOHNNY APPLETON*_____ DATE *9/14/70*
TRAINER *MARY MARINO*_____ SESSION NUMBER_____
TYPE OF RESPONSE *BEAD STRINGING* SESSION LENGTH_____

SCORE KEY: 0 = NO RESPONSE
            1 = INCORRECT RESPONSE
            2 = POOR APPROXIMATION
            3 = GOOD APPROXIMATION
            4 = EXCELLENT APPROXIMATION

TASK

STAGES	1	4	4	4	4	4				
	2	2	4	4	4	4	4			
	3	2	3	2	4	4	4	4		
	4	1	1	2	3	3	4	4	4	4	4
	5	2	3	2	2	4	4	4	4	4
	6	2	3	2	2	3	4	4	4	4	4
	7	1	1	2	1	2	1	3	2	3	3
	8									

REMARKS: *Johnny spent an average of 15 min reaching each criterion level for stages 1-3; it increased to 28 min for 4-6; + we stopped after 50 min for stage 7*

Fig. 10.10 Example of a Qualitative Data Sheet where a performance criterion is utilized.

bead-stringing program. The criterion for moving from one step to the next is that the child makes five scores of 4 in a row or in succession. As soon as he makes his fifth score of 4, he moves to the next step in the training program. However, if he accumulates three or four scores of 4, and then makes a 3 or a 2 or a 1, he must begin accumulating four scores again, since the rule is five scores of 4 in a row, uninterrupted by scores lower than 4. Notice in Fig. 10.10, that as soon as the child made his fifth score of 4 at any level of training, he immediately moved to the next training step.

A Qualitative Data Recording System is also useful for recording progress made in a Self-help Skill Training Program. It can be utilized most efficiently when all training steps in the program are clearly specified and typed on a form (as illustrated in Fig. 10.11). This type of form is designed to be used with an individual child, and can be used for fifteen training periods. This particular form is being used in our Columbus State Institute Ward Behavior Modification Project. It is used in the following manner: the trainer determines the child's level of performance, e.g., in the Eating Program, he may be able to eat with a spoon without being told to use the spoon but is messy. Therefore, he is at step 5 in the Eating Program. The next question is to decide the quality of his performance. A number of grading systems can be used. The most commonly used system is a grade of 1 or 2 with 1 indicating a poor approximation to the target behavior for that step in training, and 2 a good approximation. A five-point scoring system, such as those illustrated in Figs. 10.8, 10.9, and 10.10 could also be used. This type of form can also be used as a simple behavior checklist. The trainer simply makes a checkmark at the step the child reached in that day's training. Again, some criterion should be established for moving the child from one step in the program to the next.

*Circle a T or F in Front of Each Statement**

T F (1) When a Qualitative Data Recording System is used, the child's response or performance is graded, e.g., he gets a score of 0, 1, 2, 3, or 4.

T F (2) When a Qualitative Data Recording System is used, a tally mark is made on the data sheet to record the response or the child's performance.

T F (3) A Qualitative Data Recording System can be used to record a child's performance in an educational program, a language program, a social behavior program, a vocational program, or a self-help skill program.

T F (4) A Qualitative Data Recording System can be used *only* in an educational program.

T F (5) When programs are developed for teaching children educational,

RESIDENT'S NAME_____   MONTH_____

EATING

1. UNABLE TO FEED SELF														
2. FINGER FEEDS														
3. EATS WITH SPOON WHEN ENCOURAGED, MESSY														
4. EATS WITH SPOON WHEN ENCOURAGED, NEATLY														
5. SPOON FEEDS WITHOUT ENCOURAGEMENT, MESSY														
6. SPOON FEEDS WITHOUT ENCOURAGEMENT, NEATLY														
7. CARRIES OWN TRAY														

DRINKING

1. UNABLE TO HOLD GLASS TO DRINK														
2. DRINKS FROM GLASS BY SELF USING TWO HANDS, MESSY														
3. DRINKS FROM GLASS BY SELF USING TWO HANDS, NEATLY														
4. DRINKS FROM GLASS BY SELF USING ONE HAND, MESSY														
5. DRINKS FROM GLASS BY SELF USING ONE HAND, NEATLY														

DRESSING - PANTS

1. MAKES NO ATTEMPT														
2. PULLS PANTS UP FROM MID-THIGH														
3. PULLS PANTS UP FROM KNEES														
4. PULLS PANTS UP FROM ANKLES														
5. IF ONE FOOT OUT THROUGH PANTS, PUTS OTHER FOOT THROUGH AND PULLS PANTS UP														
6. PUTS PANTS ON UNASSISTED														

(D) T-SHIRT OR DRESS

1. UNABLE TO PULL SHIRT DOWN														
2. IF HEAD AND ARMS PUT THROUGH SHIRT, PULLS IT DOWN														
3. IF HEAD PUT THROUGH SHIRT, PUTS ARMS THROUGH, PULLS DOWN														
4. PUTS ON SHIRT WHEN HANDED IN CORRECT POSITION														
5. PUTS SHIRT ON UNASSISTED														

Fig. 10.11 Example of a Qualitative Data Sheet used to record self-help skill training.

language, social, and self-help skills, *criteria* should be established for advancing the child through various steps in the program.

T F (6) A criterion is a rule that tells us when a child should progress from one step in a training program to the next.

T F (7) The purpose of a criterion is to ensure that a child does not move on

(D) SOCKS														
1. UNABLE TO PULL SOCKS UP														
2. CAN PULL SOCKS UP AFTER BEING PULLED OVER HEEL														
3. CAN PULL SOCKS OVER HEEL														
4. CAN PUT ON SOCK IF HANDED IN CORRECT POSITION														
5. PUT ON SOCKS UNASSISTED														
(D) SHOES														
1. UNABLE TO PUT ON SHOES														
2. CAN PUT ON SHOE IF TOES HAVE ENTERED SHOE														
3. CAN PUT ON SHOES WITH MINIMAL ASSISTANCE														
4. CAN PUT ON SHOES UNASSISTED														
TEETH BRUSHING														
1. WILL NOT ALLOW TEETH TO BE BRUSHED														
2. ALLOWS TEETH TO BE BRUSHED														
3. BRUSHES WITH ASSISTANCE														
4. PUTS TOOTH PASTE ON AND BRUSHES UNASSISTED														
TOILETING														
1. WILL NOT SIT ON TOILET														
2. UNAWARE OF HAVING SOILED OR WET														
3. HAS AWARENESS OF HAVING SOILED OR WET														
4. USES TOILET IF BROUGHT THERE														
5. INDICATES HAVING TO USE TOILET														
6. GOES TO TOILET BY SELF TO DEFECATE OR URINATE														
7. USES TOILET AND FLUSHES IT														
U-D SOCKS														
1. UNABLE TO PULL SOCK OFF FROM TOE														
2. PULLS SOCK OFF FROM TOE														
3. PULLS SOCK OFF FROM OVER HEEL														
4. PULLS SOCKS OFF UNASSISTED														

Fig. 10.11   (*Continued*).

from one step in a training program to the next too soon, but also moves from step to step as quickly as possible.

T F (8) The purpose of a criterion is to move a child through a training program as slowly as possible.

Answers are on page 139.

U-D SHOES															
1. UNABLE TO TAKE OFF SHOE EVEN WHEN PARTIALLY TAKEN OFF															
2. TAKES OR KICKS OFF SHOE WHEN PARTIALLY TAKEN OFF															
3. TAKES OFF SHOES															
U-D PANTS															
1. UNABLE TO TAKE OFF PANTS FROM ANKLES															
2. TAKES OFF PANTS FROM ANKLES															
3. TAKES OF PANTS FROM KNEES															
4. TAKES OFF PANTS FROM MID-THIGH															
5. TAKES OFF PANTS FROM WAIST															
U-D T-SHIRT OR DRESS															
1. UNABLE TO TAKE SHIRT OFF FROM WRIST															
2. TAKES SHIRT OFF FROM WRIST															
3. TAKES SHIRT OFF FROM ONE ARM															
4. TAKES SHIRT OFF FROM BOTH ARMS															
5. TAKES SHIRT OFF FROM HEAD AND ARMS															
6. TAKES SHIRT OFF UNASSISTED															
BATHING															
1. UNABLE TO HANDLE WASH CLOTH OR SOAP															
2. CAN ADEQUATELY SOAP AND WASH HANDS															
3. CAN ADEQUATELY HOLD RAG															
4. CAN ADEQUATELY SOAP RAG AND WASH FACE															
DRYING															
1. UNABLE TO HANDLE TOWEL FOR DRYING															
2. CAN DRY HANDS															
3. CAN DRY FACE															

Fig. 10.11   (*Continued*).

DIAGNOSING BEHAVIOR

The purpose of the Diagnostic Data Recording Procedure is to *identify the causes of undesirable behavior* so they can be eliminated. There are usually two things that make undesirable behavior occur: (1) a stimulus or condition that immediately precedes the behavior and triggers it, and (2) some condition that reinforces it once it does occur, increases its occurrence and maintains it. The Diagnostic Data Recording Procedure is designed to identify these two things. As Fig. 10.12 indicates, there is a

DIAGNOSIS OF UNDESIRABLE BEHAVIOR

TYPE OF PROGRAM *STOP HEADBANGING* SCORE_____
PATIENT_ *BILLY   MINOSOTO* ___ DATE_ *9/14/70*
TRAINER_ *MARY MAXWELL* __ SESSION NUMBER_ *8*__
TYPE OF RESPONSE_ *Hd Bng* _____ SESSION LENGTH_____

BEHAVIOR	WHAT PRECEDED IT	WHAT FOLLOWED IT
Headbang	*Jinny M. hit him*	*Restraints + scolding*
"	*I told him to sweep*	" " "
"	*I took his tray*	" " "
"	*He asked + said "No"*	" " "
"	*?*	" " "

REMARKS:

Fig. 10.12   Example of a Diagnostic Data Sheet.

space on the data sheet to identify the undesirable behavior, a second space to record the event that immediately preceded the behavior, and a third space to record what happened when the behavior occurred or what followed it. Each time the undesirable behavior occurs, the trainer records what was happening just before it occurred. In the first entry, Billy M. was hit by Jinny M. just before he started headbanging. Then, the trainer records what happened after the child began headbanging. In Fig. 10.12, he was restrained and scolded. The behavior is observed a number of times, and each time the trainer records what preceded it and what followed it. Then she searches for a pattern. In this example, it appears that a frustrating experience always precedes and apparently triggers or causes headbanging to occur, while restraint and scolding may be reinforcing and maintaining this type of behavior and subsequently increasing its intensity and duration.

Circle a T or F in Front of Each Statement*
T   F   (1) A Diagnostic Data Recording Procedure is used to identify the causes of undesirable behavior so that they can be eliminated.

T   F   (2) A Diagnostic Data Recording Procedure is used to determine how well a child is learning a target behavior in an educational, language, social, vocational or self-help skill program.

T   F   (3) Two things that usually cause undesirable behavior are: (a) a stimulus or condition that immediately precedes the behavior, and (b) some condition that reinforces it once it occurs.

T   F   (4) Two things that usually cause undesirable behavior are: (a) a stimulus or condition that immediately precedes it, and (b) a second condition that precedes it as well.

Answers are on page 139.

SUMMARY

There are four kinds of data recording procedures: frequency, duration, qualitative, and diagnostic. The *frequency* procedure is the *simplest* type of data recording procedure. It is nothing more than a *tally system*. This procedure can be used to record bowel and bladder elimination, aggressive behavior, temper tantrums, or "hyperactivity" such as a child jumping up out of his seat and running around a classroom. A *duration* recording procedure is used when we want to know *how long* some particular behavior lasted or how long it has been since it occurred. This technique can be used to evaluate temper tantrums, self-destructive behavior, or how long a child can sit or work at a task uninterrupted. The *Qualitative Data Recording Procedure* provides a *grade* for a response. The child performs a task and receives a grade on the task, e.g., 0, 1, 2, 3, or 4. This is a highly useful recording procedure that not only tells us how many times the behavior of interest occurred, but also indicates how well the child performed each time. This procedure is very useful for evaluating performance in educational, language, social, vocational, and self-help skill programs. The *diagnostic* data procedure is used to *identify the causes of undesirable behavior* so that they can be eliminated.

*Fill in the Missing Words**

   (1) Data collection systems are needed in a training program so that we can accurately and reliably _____ whether the child is getting better or worse or is making no progress at all.

   (2) Without an objective data system, we _____ accurately and reliably determine progress made by the child in the training program.

   (3) A Frequency Data Recording Procedure utilizes a _____ _____.

   (4) By substituting a _____ _____ and a

_____ _____, the Frequency Data Recording Procedure provides a highly useful technique for evaluating a toilet training program.

(5) A Duration Data Recording Procedure is used to record how _____ _____ _____ or how _____ _____ _____ _____ _____ behavior occurred.

(6) When a Qualitative Data Recording Procedure is used, the child's response is _____.

(7) A _____ is a rule that tells us when a child should progress from one step in a training program to the next.

(8) When programs are developed for teaching children educational, language, social, and self-help skills, _____ should be established for advancing the child through various steps in the program.

(9) A _____ Data Recording Procedure is used to identify the causes of undesirable behavior so that they can be eliminated.

(10) Two things that usually cause _____ _____ are: (a) a stimulus or condition that immediately precedes it, and (b) some condition that reinforces it when it occurs.

Answers are on pages 139–140.

Answer These Questions
(1) Why are data recording procedures important to behavior modification programs?
(2) Describe a Frequency Data Recording Procedure.
(3) When would you use a Frequency Data Recording Procedure?
(4) Describe a Duration Data Recording Procedure.
(5) When would you use a Duration Data Recording Procedure?
(6) Describe a Qualitative Data Recording Procedure.
(7) When would you use a Qualitative Data Recording Procedure?
(8) What is a criterion? Why are criteria used in training programs?
(9) Describe a Diagnostic Data Recording Procedure.
(10) When would you use a Diagnostic Data Recording Procedure?

Answers are on page 140.

Answers to T-F, Fill-in, and Essay Questions

T-F on page 119
    (1) T
    (2) F
    (3) T

T-F on page 124
    (1) F
    (2) T
    (3) T
    (4) F
    (5) T

T-F on page 128
    (1) F
    (2) T
    (3) T

T-F on pages 132–134
    (1) T
    (2) F
    (3) T
    (4) F
    (5) T
    (6) T
    (7) T
    (8) F

T-F on pages 136–137
    (1) T
    (2) F
    (3) T
    (4) F

Fill-in on pages 137–138
    (1) determine
    (2) cannot
    (3) tally system

(4)   coded letter; time entry
(5)   long behavior lasted; long it has been since
(6)   graded
(7)   criterion
(8)   criteria
(9)   diagnostic
(10)   undesirable behavior

Essay Questions on page 138

(1)   Data recording procedures are important to behavior modification programs because they enable us to accurately and reliably determine the influence of our treatment program on the child's behavior.

(2)   A Frequency Data Recording Procedure uses a tally system. The trainer makes a mark on a sheet of paper each time a response occurs.

(3)   A Frequency Data Recording Procedure can be used to record toileting behavior, aggressive behavior, temper tantrums, and "hyperactivity," e.g., a child repeatedly jumps up from his seat at a table in a classroom.

(4)   A Duration Data Recording Procedure records how long a particular kind of behavior lasts or how long it has been since the behavior occurred.

(5)   A Duration Data Recording Procedure could be used to record temper tantrums, self-destructive behavior, and how long a child will sit and work at a task uninterrupted or without jumping up from his seat.

(6)   A Qualitative Data Recording Procedure provides the child with a grade for his response or his behavior.

(7)   A Qualitative Data Recording Procedure can be used to evaluate educational, social, language, vocational, and self-help skill training programs.

(8)   A criterion is a rule that tells us when the child should progress from one step in a training program to the next. Criteria are used so that the child does not progress from one step in the program to the next too soon, i.e., before he is ready to, but also moves from step to step as quickly as possible.

(9)   A Diagnostic Data Recording Procedure records two things that can make undesirable behavior occur: (a) the situation that immediately preceded the occurrence of the undesirable behavior (the possible stimulus that triggers the undesirable behavior), and (b) the events that followed the occurrence of the undesirable behavior (conditions that can reinforce or maintain the undesirable behavior).

(10)   A Diagnostic Data Recording Procedure is used when a trainer wishes to determine what is causing undesirable behavior so that he can eliminate it.

Glossary

Behavior Modification. A discipline of psychotherapy, primarily concerned with changing observed behavior.

Bridging Signal. A bridge between the completion of the behavior being shaped and the presentation of the main reinforcement.

Chaining. A shaping technique used to teach a retardate a complex behavioral unit, such as dressing, one component at a time. Each behavioral component can be thought of as a link that makes up the behavioral chain.

Contingent Reinforcement. The thing a person has to do or the behavior a person has to carry out to get the reinforcement.

Extinction. Ignoring someone when he does something you do not want him to do. Not giving reinforcement.

Fading. Gradually changing a stimulus. If a new stimulus is gradually introduced, this is called *fading in* a stimulus, and if a stimulus is gradually removed, this is *fading out* a stimulus.

Incompatible Response. Response which prevents another behavior from occurring, because the two cannot occur simultaneously.

Operant Behavior. Behavior under a person's voluntary control. It is called operant behavior because it operates on the environment to provide the person with reinforcement or rewards, such as food, water, money, warmth, and entertainment.

Operant Conditioning. Conditioning or training that is limited primarily to changing voluntary behavior in people, such as walking, talking, and doing things with the hands, as opposed to reflexive behavior, such as eye blink, salivation, and digestion.

Operant Level.   Behavioral level before training is begun, i.e., the behavior of interest to the trainer.

Prompting.   Introducing a cue for the purpose of more clearly communicating with a child. There are three kinds of prompts: verbal, gestural, and physical.

Punishment.   Something which either decelerates or stops behavior.

Reinforcement.   Something a person likes, e.g., a reward, that "turns him on"; he is also willing to work to get it.

Shaping.   Molding or developing simple behavior into complex behavior.

Stimulus Control.   Cues, stimuli, or parts of the environment that control a person's behavior or make it occur.

Stimulus Generalization.   *See* "Transfer of Training."

Successive Approximation.   A shaping technique used to teach a retardate a single piece of behavior or component in a step-by-step fashion, e.g., putting on a shirt or a pair of pants or socks or shoes or eating with a spoon.

Transfer of Training.   Generalization of behavior learned from one location or situation to another.

References

Azrin, N. H. and Holz, W. C., Punishment. In Honig, W. K. (ed.) *Operant Behavior: Areas of Research and Application.* New York: Appleton-Century-Crofts, 1966.

Baer, D. M. and Wolf, M. F., The entry into natural communities of reinforcement. In Ulrich, R., Stachnik, T., and Mabry, J. (eds.) *Control of Human Behavior: From Cure to Prevention.* Glenview, Illinois: Scott Foresman and Company, 1970.

Bensberg, G. J., *Teaching the Mentally Retarded.* Atlanta Southern Regional Education Board, 1965.

Bijou, S. W. A functional analysis of retarded development. In Ellis, N. R. (ed.) *International Review of Research in Mental Retardation.* New York: Academic Press, 1966.

Browning, R. M. and Stover, D. O. *Behavior Modification in Child Treatment.* Chicago: Aldine-Atherton, 1971.

Bucher, B. and Lovaas, O. I. Use of aversive stimulation in behavior modification. In Jones, M. R. (ed.) *Miami Symposium on the Prediction of Behavior 1967: Aversive Stimulation.* Miami: University of Miami Press, 1966.

Ferster, C. B., Positive reinforcement and behavioral deficits of autistic children. *Child Development,* 1961, **32**, 437–456.

Ferster, C. B., Classification of behavioral pathology. In Krasner, L. and Ullmann, L. P. (eds.) *Research in Behavior Modification.* New York: Holt, Rinehart and Winston, Inc., 1965.

Ferster, C. B., Arbitrary and natural reinforcement. *The Psychological Record,* 1967, **17**, 341–347.

Ferster, C. B. and Perrott, M. C., *Behavior Principles.* New York: New Century, Meredith Publishing Company, 1968.

Ferster, C. B. and Skinner, B. F., *Schedules of Reinforcement.* New York: Appleton-Century-Crofts, 1957.

Gardner, W. I., *Behavior Modification in Mental Retardation: The Education of the Mentally Retarded Adolescent and Adult.* Chicago: Aldine-Atherton, 1971.

Honig, W. K. (ed.) *Operant Behavior: Areas of Research and Application.* New York: Appleton-Century-Crofts, 1966.

Lent, J. R., LeBlanc, J., and Spradlin, J. E., Designing a rehabilitative culture for moderately retarded adolescent girls. In Ulrich, R., Stachnik, T., and Mabry, J. (eds.) *Control of Human Behavior: From Cure to Prevention.* Glenview, Illinois: Scott, Foresman and Company, 1970.

Lovaas, O. I. *Behavior Modification: Teaching Language to Psychotic Children*, (16mm movie). New York: Appleton-Century-Crofts, 1969.

Patterson, G. R., *Families*. Champaign, Illinois: Research Press, 1971.

Patterson, G. R. and Gullion, M. E., *Living with Children*. Champaign, Illinois: Research Press, 1968.

Premack, D. Toward empirical behavioral laws: I. Positive reinforcement. *Psychological Review*, 1959, **66**, 219–233.

Premack, D., Reinforcement theory, In Levine, D. (ed.) *Nebraska Symposium on Motivation*. Lincoln, Nebraska: University of Nebraska Press, 1965.

Reese, E. P., *The Analysis of Human Operant Behavior*. Dubuque, Iowa: William C. Brown Company, 1966.

Sidman, M. and Stoddard, L., Programming perception and learning for retarded children. In Ellis, N. R. (ed.) *International Review of Mental Retardation*. New York: Academic Press, 1967.

Skinner, B. F., *Science and Human Behavior*. New York: MacMillan, 1953.

Skinner, B. F., *Verbal Behavior*. New York: Appleton-Century-Crofts, 1957.

Skinner, B. F., *The Technology of Teaching*. New York: Appleton-Century-Crofts, 1968.

Spradlin, J. E. and Giradeau, F. L., The behavior of moderately and severely retarded persons. In Ellis, N. R. (ed.) *International Review of Research in Mental Retardation*. New York: Academic Press, 1966.

Szasz, T., The myth of mental illness. In Milton, O. and Wahler, R. G. (eds.) *Behavior Disorders: Perspectives and Trends*. New York: Lippincott Company, 1969.

Terrace, H. S., Stimulus control. In Honig, W. K. (ed.) *Operant Behavior: Areas of Research and Application*. New York: Appleton-Century-Crofts, 1966.

Trabasso, T. and Bower, G. H., *Attention in Learning: Theory and Research*. New York: John Wiley and Sons, Inc., 1968.

Ullmann, L. P. and Krasner, L. *Case Studies in Behavior Modification*. New York: Holt, Rinehart and Winston, Inc., 1965, pp. 1–63.

Watson, L. S., Applications of operant conditioning techniques to institutionalized severely and profoundly retarded children. *Mental Retardation Abstracts*, 1967, **4**, 1–18.

Watson, L. S., Behavior modification of residents and personnel in institutions for the mentally retarded. In Baumeister, A. A. and Butterfield, E. (eds.) *Residential Facilities for the Mentally Retarded*. Chicago: Aldine Publishing Company, 1970.

Zeaman, D. and House, B. J., The role of attention in retardate discrimination. In Ellis, N. R. (ed.) *Handbook of Mental Deficiency*. New York: McGraw-Hill, 1963.

Index

Page numbers in italic refer to tables.

145

TITLES IN THE PERGAMON GENERAL PSYCHOLOGY SERIES